Black Theatre
in the
1960s and 1970s

Recent Titles in
Contributions in Afro-American and African Studies
Series Advisers: John W. Blassingame and Henry Louis Gates, Jr.

Voices from Under: Black Narrative in Latin America and the Caribbean
William Luis, editor

Contemporary Public Policy Perspectives and Black Americans: Issues in an Era of Retrenchment Politics
Mitchell F. Rice and Woodrow Jones, Jr., editors

Student Culture and Activism in Black South African Universities: The Roots of Resistance
Mokubung O. Nkomo

The Cinema of Ousmane Sembene, A Pioneer of African Film
Françoise Pfaff

Philanthropy and Jim Crow in American Social Science
John H. Stanfield

Israel in the Black American Perspective
Robert G. Weisbord and Richard Kazarian, Jr.

African Culture: The Rhythms of Unity
Molefi Kete Asante and Kariamu Welsh Asante, editors

Writing "Independent" History: African Historiography, 1960–1980
Caroline Neale

More Than Drumming: Essays on African and Afro-Latin American Music and Musicians
Irene V. Jackson, editor

More Than Dancing: Essays on Afro-American Music and Musicians
Irene V. Jackson, editor

Sterling A. Brown: Building the Black Aesthetic Tradition
Joanne V. Gabbin

Amalgamation!: Race, Sex, and Rhetoric in the Nineteenth-Century American Novel
James Kinney

Black Theatre in the 1960s and 1970s

A HISTORICAL-CRITICAL ANALYSIS OF THE MOVEMENT

Mance Williams

CONTRIBUTIONS IN AFRO-AMERICAN AND
AFRICAN STUDIES, NUMBER 87

Greenwood Press
WESTPORT, CONNECTICUT
LONDON, ENGLAND

Library of Congress Cataloging in Publication Data

Williams, Mance.
  Black theatre in the 1960s and 1970s.

  (Contributions in Afro-American and African
studies, ISSN 0069-0624 ; no. 87)
  Bibliography: p.
  Includes index.
  1. Afro-American theater—History—20th century.
2. American drama—Afro-American authors—History and
criticism.   3. American drama—20th century—History
and criticism.   I. Title.   II. Series.
PN2270.A35W54   1985   792'.08996073   84-22506
ISBN 0-313-23835-9 (lib. bdg.)

Library of Congress Catalog Card Number: 84-22506
ISBN: 0-313-23835-9
ISSN: 0069-0624

First published in 1985

Greenwood Press
A Division of Congressional Information Service, Inc.
88 Post Road West
Westport, Connecticut 06881

Printed in the United States of America

10 9 8 7 6 5 4 3 2 1

In Memory of My Grandmother
Mrs. Larry Williams

Contents

Black Theatre
in the
1960s and 1970s

Introduction

The Black Theatre Movement of the 1960s and 1970s was essentially a populist movement. Its alignment with the broader-based Civil Rights and Black Power Movements gives it an attitude and temperament opposite to that of the "traditional" Black Theatre. Doris E. Abramson, in her study of Black playwrights in the American theatre from 1925 to 1959, writes, "The plays seem to be mainly concerned with the individual Negro's problem of being assimilated into or revolting against the dominant white society."[1] In the study Abramson does a creditable job of analyzing the situation in which Blacks in the American theatre, and playwrights especially, have always found themselves. She examines the works of certain acknowledged playwrights in terms of the social, political, and economic conditions in the United States. While this approach is undertaken with genuine interest and seriousness, it still manifests the major constraint that limits much of the criticism done by Whites (and many Blacks, too) of Black literary works. In many ways it appears that conventional historical-critical methodology contains built-in preconceptions and slanted value-judgments. The attitude and approach taken by the majority of White critics toward Black writing is summarized in David Littlejohn's *White on Black: A Critical Survey of Writings by American Negroes*. First, Black writers are obsessed with the subject of White oppression, concludes Littlejohn. Second, they have not yet reached a sufficient level of competence to be judged on a level with White writers. Furthermore, because Black writers are incapable of perceiving beyond their extreme color consciousness, they lack a universal perspective. Littlejohn states:

> It may one day be different, but a white American today will find it an exhausting and depressing enterprise to immerse himself for long in the recent literature of the American Negro—for a number of reasons. Much of the writing, like much of the writing of any race, is simply poor, the product of small minds that happen to be Negro. But aesthetic pain is a minor pain; more dispiriting is the simple experience of dwelling in the dull dark prison yard that is so often the Negro writer's world. . . . Economic oppression, dehumanization, ignominious role playing, the constant dealings with the very bottom of the human heap—the responding spirit is dulled, finally, bored by the iteration of hopelessness, the sordid limitation of the soul in the tight closet of black imagination.[2]

Granted, not all White criticism of Black writing is as opinionated and negative as Littlejohn's, but the fact that Littlejohn is a respected critic gives his views credibility. Robert Bone's attempt in *The Negro Novel in America* to analyze Black writing by using "formal literary criticism" was criticized by Littlejohn as "somehow fidgety, uncomfortably precious."[3] The sharp disagreement between these two critical views highlights the dilemma White critics face when it comes to agreeing on a fair and equitable approach to the evaluation of Black writing.

It was, to be sure, a constant complaint of the Black Theatre playwrights that their works were not being evaluated fairly or competently by establishment critics. They wanted more Black critics. It could be that this position eventually succeeded in "turning off" some potential non-Black critics who might have wanted to author studies of the Black Theatre Movement, for prior to the present study, no attempt has been made to provide a strictly historical-critical analysis of the Black Theatre Movement of the 1960s to the 1970s. However, there have been several works written on Amiri Baraka that include examinations of his theatrical contributions.[4] One of these studies, *Baraka: The Renegade and the Mask* by Kimberly W. Benston, attempts to justify the use of a traditional model of literary criticism by "elevating" Baraka into the ranks of European literary "greats." Another interesting approach was taken by Werner

Sollors in his book *Amiri Baraka/LeRoi Jones: The Quest for a "Populist Modernism."* Sollors portrays Baraka as a hero to Black people in their struggle for social and political justice, and as a leading contributor to modern avant-garde literature. More importantly, Theodore R. Hudson in his work *From LeRoi Jones to Amiri Baraka* provides valuable insights into the literary uses of Black Consciousness and the Black Aesthetic. Harold Cruse's *The Crisis of the Negro Intellectual* takes up the subject of the new Black drama of the 1960s and 1970s and devotes an entire chapter-essay to the subject: "The Harlem Black Arts Theatre—New Dialogue with the Lost Generation." Cruse's acerbic wit and caustic criticism in this and other essays on the theatre are sometimes distracting; nonetheless, he offers some enlightening perspectives on the Black Theatre Movement. Regrettably, he too spends an inordinate amount of time on the eccentricities and novelty of Baraka, thereby restricting the scope of his coverage.

Other recent works on the Black Theatre should be mentioned. *The Theatre of Black Americans*, two volumes of critical essays edited by Erroll Hill, gives a comprehensive overview of the historic and aesthetic development of Black Theatre as an art form. Paul Carter Harrison's *The Drama of Nommo* discusses the influence African culture has had in shaping a unique African-American aesthetic and philosophical approach to life. Although Black Theatre is treated extensively, Harrison focuses on the "Africanness" pervasive throughout all aspects of Black American life. *Black Theatre: Present Condition* by Woodie King, Jr., is a compilation of previously published essays and interviews that express the views and recount the experiences of this leading Black theatre producer.

Of course, the Black Theatre Movement, both at the height of its public interest and today, has garnered its share of critical and descriptive writings, especially in magazine articles and introductions to anthologies. In fact, taken as a whole, these writings comprise a rather sizable body of criticism. During its existence, *Black World* provided a rich outlet for essays by a new generation of Black Theatre–oriented critics, and several anthologies bring together some of the best writing on the subject. Those that deserve mention are *Black Expression; The Black*

American Writer, Volume II: Poetry and Drama; and *The Black Aesthetic.* And while *Black Drama* by playwright Loften Mitchell offers some insights into the causes and moods attending the Black Theatre Movement of the 1960s, the book's importance is primarily in its historical analysis. Also, Abramson's *Negro Playwrights in the American Theatre, 1925–1959* includes a "look at" the new playwrights; unfortunately, this portion of the book forms an epilogue and is not benefited by a substantial body of published works upon which to draw.

It would appear, then, that any guidelines used to analyze plays from the Black Theatre Movement must be broader than those that have traditionally been used. Therefore, in view of the purposes and goals expressed by the movement's leading spokesmen, and in recognition of certain contradictions and counter-tendencies, any examination of the Black Theatre Movement of the 1960s–1970s should reflect at least three critical approaches: (1) that of the Marxist, (2) that of the structuralist, and (3) that of realism/naturalism.

The Marxist approach is based mainly on Sergei Eisenstein's dialectical methodology for analyzing film form. Eisenstein cites conflict as the basis for all works of art and all art forms. He declares:

It is art's task to make manifest the contradictions of Being . . . by forming equitable views by stirring up contradictions within the spectator's mind, and to forge accurate intellectual concepts from the dynamic clash of opposing passions.[5]

Within the Black Theatre, the Black Consciousness plays, rather than the Black Revolutionary plays, successfully used the dialectical approach by confronting Blacks with the negative aspects of their consciousness and prescribing more positive alternatives. The purpose was to build a stronger and more militant psychology to offset a defeatist psychology conditioned by a history of forced servitude, discrimination, and racial denigration. A Marxist approach to criticism must focus on the development of a Black Consciousness in terms of four stages: (1) accusation and condemnation, (2) awareness and acceptance, (3) commitment, and (4) action. Black Revolutionary plays are distinguished from Black Consciousness plays if the action stage is accompanied by a direct "call to arms." In other words, it is assumed that the development of a positive Black Consciousness is a prerequisite to armed revolt.

A few playwrights, such as Edgar White and Adrienne Kennedy, are highly original and individualistic. Their works, marked by deliberate, self-conscious preoccupation with style and structure, demand a structurally oriented critical approach. This approach is needed since these playwrights are also prone to explore freely the elements of myth and ritual. Conversely, their plays reflect the structuralist's view that we shape the world through our consciousness.[6] A structuralist approach to criticism, then, should pose the following questions: (1) Is the playwright preoccupied with artistic concerns of form and style rather than the explicit social messages and polemics? (2) Are myth and ritual dominant forces in the playwright's dramaturgy? (3) Is the playwright concerned with portraying the different states of consciousness, and with creating tension in the audience by having its sense of reality sharply conflict with the reality portrayed on stage?

Although many Black plays succeed in projecting a sense of Black Consciousness thematically, they still reflect styles of realism and naturalism. In such cases, their analysis needs to take into account the subject matter, theme, and believability of character and setting. When applied to these plays, traditional critical standards of realism and naturalism prove insufficient, however. Dramatic interpretation of the Black Experience, depicted especially in plays such as *In the Wine Time* and *The Fabulous Miss Marie* by Ed Bullins, strives for a graphic depiction of Black life that transcends imitative stage realism. Supposedly, the characters in these plays and the actors who portray them have so much in common that little playacting is needed. This concept focuses on the premise that the experiences of the playwright, the actors, and the characters in the play are derived from the same source and are virtually identical in content. Furthermore, advocates of this trend in Black Theatre demand that theatre realism be stretched to its furthest limits of believability. Members of the audience, stress these advocates, need to confront reality, not to try to escape it by insisting on, and being given, manufactured fantasy or a fictitious past. The realism/naturalism approach, therefore, poses the inclusive question, Has the playwright presented an accurate description of the Black Experience?

To qualify as a significant record and evaluation of the Black Theatre Movement, this study focuses not only on the playwrights but on the important theatre companies, their formation, productions, and performers; it also covers the role and contributions of the Black producers. It is clear that specific questions, and answers, lie as much in the history of the movement as in the critical analysis of the plays. Questions germane to the study on the Black Theatre are: Can the movement be shown to present a coherent, unified body of dramatic works and productions that can be evaluated by the application of a proper aesthetic, historical, and dialectical criterion? Does the Black Theatre Movement of the 1960s and 1970s rest on a distinct, viable aesthetic, or does the movement—creatively and philosophically—follow more of a dialectical approach? Is the Black Theatre Movement a unique entity, or is it merely a species of a larger genus? In other words, does it have anything in common with the other radical, innovative movements of the same epoch, i.e., Off-Off Broadway, the Living Theatre, the Radical Theatre, the Performance Group, etc.? However, the inevitable and central question that this study must address is, How, and in what manner, does the Black Theatre Movement of the 1960s and 1970s break with or continue trends of Black-written and Black-produced theatre begun in America as early as 1821–22?

NOTES

1. Doris E. Abramson, *Negro Playwrights in the American Theatre, 1925–1959* (New York: Columbia University Press, 1969), p. 4.

2. David Littlejohn, *Black on White: A Critical Survey of Writings by American Negroes* (New York: Grossman Publishers, 1966), p. 4.

3. Ibid.

4. In 1966 LeRoi Jones adopted the name Imamu (Spiritual Leader) Ameer Baraka (Blessed Prince). He later began using Amiri without any change in meaning. Amiri Baraka is used in this work unless ref-

erence is made to plays and productions in the 1960s when he still used the name Jones.

5. Sergei Eisenstein, *Film Form* (New York: Harcourt, Brace and World/A Harvest Book, 1949), p. 47.

6. Allan Casebier, *Film Appreciation* (New York: Harcourt Brace Jovanovich, 1976), p. 162.

1

The Black Theatre Movement: Expression of a New Mood

In a way, it can be said that the Black Theatre Movement of the 1960s and 1970s began in Paris when a Black actor asked Jean Genet to write a play for an all-Black cast. The French playwright replied: "But what exactly is a Black? First of all, what's his color?"[1]

The problem for Genet, though complex, was no doubt as ontological as aesthetic. For although he was an outcast, Genet had first to identify with the Black frame of reference. He had to define, for his own creative purpose, the Black Experience. Not that Black—in terms of defining human essence and existence—is an abstract concept. The Black actor perplexed Genet by being so specific in his request. Questions triggered by that request would be: What is so different about a play for Blacks that it has to be treated with special artistic consideration? Must a whole new aesthetic be created; a whole new consciousness be developed; Blackness be redefined in terms of human existence, essence, and experience? Genet's answer, if that is what he realized within *The Blacks*, merely reiterated stereotypical images and attitudes; the same old Blacks with a new anger. Still, the questions were important and destined to become a predominant intellectual and artistic concern during the decade of the 1960s and beyond.

But exactly when, where, and from whom did the idea for the development of a Black Theatre come? Like the process of communication itself, the idea reflects a continuous human need to adapt to a changing, hostile environment. Indeed, with the creation of the African Grove Theatre in 1821–22, Black theatre craftsmen had begun to realize that if a Black audience was to be built, and actors and playwrights of color given a chance to learn and develop, then Blacks were going to have to form their own "alternative" theatres. Therefore, it can be inferred that a Black Theatre movement of sorts began as far back as 1821–22 as an "entertainment" venture by a Mr. Brown and actor James Hewlett.[2] However, these gentlemen probably had no conscious intention of merging philosophy and aesthetics into a separate and viable Black Theatre. Something on the order of a purposeful movement to create an institutionalized Black Theatre emerged around 1915 with the Anita Bush Stock Company, later known as the Lafayette Players. Located in the heart of the Black community, Cleveland's Karamu House was organized in 1916 by Russell and Rowena Jellife. For the purpose of staging Ridgeley Torrence's *Three Plays for a Negro Theatre*, the Hapgood Coloured Players were organized in 1917. But perhaps the most sustained movement to develop viable Black theatres spans the years between 1923 and 1940. In Chicago the Ethiopian Art Theatre was formed in 1923, and W. E. B. Du Bois founded the Krigway Players in Harlem in 1926. In 1928 Jesse Fawcett helped organize the Harlem Experimental Theatre. In 1929 the Negro Art Theatre, the Harlem Community Players, and the Dunbar Garden Players were founded.[3] Langston Hughes spearheaded the Harlem Suitcase Theatre in 1937; one year later Dick Campbell and his wife, Muriel Rahn, formed the Rose McClendon Players. And in 1940 Abram Hill and Frederick O'Neal organized the American Negro Theatre.

Certainly the minstrel phenomenon and the Black musicals of the 1890s and 1920s influenced the history of the Black Theatre Movement. In *Black Manhattan* James Weldon Johnson divides the Black Theatre into three phases. Phase one begins around 1865 with the founding of the Georgia Minstrels by Charles Hicks. Often denigrated by exponents of Black Pride during the 1960s and 1970s, minstrelsy was the Black performer's first big break into professional American theatre. Phase two dates from Sam T. Jack's 1890 *Creole Show*, when the Afro-American freed himself of the minstrel tradition and its plantation stigma. Modest innovations introduced in the *Creole Show* inspired greater achievements in musical comedy. According to

Johnson, phase three began with the migration of Blacks from the downtown theatres of Manhattan to the uptown theatres of Harlem, around 1910. Except for a hiatus caused by the First World War, this period lasted through the 1920s and seems to have expired with the Harlem Renaissance during the Depression. Still, there was more Black theatrical activity from 1910 to 1930 than from 1945 to 1960. Subsequently, during the early part of the 1960s, with the evolution of Black-centered consciousness and its philosophical and psychological weltanschauung, Black Art, including Black Theatre, attempted by aggressively asserting its own identity and values to become not just a parallel medium but a revolutionary movement.

According to Stuart W. Little in his book *Off-Broadway: The Prophetic Theatre*, "Genet's play *The Blacks* was the real beginning of Black Theatre."[4] Whether or not this statement is completely accurate, *The Blacks* (1959) does stand as a milestone in the history of the "New Black Theatre." Besides showcasing Black actors and giving them steady work for a while, the play demonstrated the power inherent in ritual drama and showed producers that a new White audience had arrived. Also, *The Blacks* was important in opening vistas for the eventual birth of more radical theatre forms that were to be therapeutic and participatory. Nonetheless, the consensus among Black Theatre scholars is that the Black Theatre Movement of the 1960s and 1970s began with the first production of LeRoi Jones' *Dutchman* in 1964. Another Jones play, *The Slave*, was also produced in 1964 and is just as important to the period as *Dutchman*. In spite of their racially explicit content, these plays reiterated the popular intellectual subject matter of the day and served the same audience as *The Blacks*. Both *Dutchman* and *The Slave* confront the problems of the outsider in society and the dilemma faced by the artist-intellectual and his commitment to the masses. Much like James Baldwin's *Blues for Mister Charlie*, Jones' plays try to probe deep into the psychic phenomenon of the American racial ontology. As catalysts, they provided an incentive to Jones to seek a positive, creative, and intellectual act by exiling himself to a wholly Black environment and experience. It was, therefore, with Jones' move to Harlem in 1965 and his founding of the Harlem Black Arts Repertory Theatre School that the

Black Arts wing of the Black Theatre Movement was begun. This wing was indeed the most provocative and innovative within the movement, but it was not the only influence.

Three disparate but interrelated influences accompanied the Black Theatre Movement. Although the entire movement was rooted in the Civil Rights Movement, the Free Southern Theatre was the standard-bearer throughout the Deep South. Organized in 1964 by members of the Student Nonviolent Coordinating Committee (SNCC), the Free Southern Theater planned to use theatre as a means of educating and politicizing Blacks in the rural South. They decided that Black people could be reached more easily through plays than literature and books, a dictum voiced later by Baraka. On the other hand, the Negro Ensemble Company (NEC) wanted to counteract the practice of the White theatre establishment, both commercial and non-commercial, of slighting Black artists. Theirs was the time-worn problem of racial exclusion of the professional experienced by Blacks in all areas of life throughout America. Thus, when NEC was organized in 1967 in New York, it continued a trend begun by the Anita Bush Players in 1915 and carried on by the American Negro Theatre of the 1940s. Essentially, this was the need for Black theatre artists to organize themselves to combat racism and to assume control over their destiny. In this respect, they were taking part in the Civil Rights struggle, but their main concern was the survival of Blacks in the theatre arts rather than total liberation of the race. Whatever its criticism for not engaging more actively in protest theatre, NEC did eventually come to embrace the idea of Black plays by Black playwrights for a predominantly Black audience. The Negro Ensemble Company's contribution to the Black Theatre Movement is manifested in its development of actors, playwrights, and technical theatre personnel who continue to perpetuate Black professional involvement in theatre.

In 1969 a group of four one-act plays under the collective title *A Black Quartet* opened at a theatre in New York City, and the opening turned out to be an event of curious significance. The Black Power Movement was at its zenith by 1969. Black plays written by Black playwrights were no longer a novelty on the American stage, especially in the city of New York. There were either permanent Black theatres or itinerant Black drama groups springing up in most major northern cities as well as a few urban centers in the southern states. The names of certain young Black playwrights were included on credible "who's who" lists of America's best and brightest young dramatists. LeRoi Jones and Ed Bullins were names to drop if one wanted to display an awareness of contemporary American theatre. So what was so special about the production of a group of one-act plays, especially when three of the playwrights (Jones, Bullins, and Ron Milner) had already been introduced to theatre consumers? It was that for the first time the Black Theatre Movement was shown to be viable and cohesive. This particular production was designed to demonstrate that indeed a serious revolt among a sizable segment of Black Theatre artists was taking place on stage. In the introduction to the printed collection, critic Clayton Riley explains, "The plays contained here—under the collective title *The Black Quartet*—can serve to define a mood and movement."[5]

The authors of these four plays differ in temperament but not in mood. That mood has as its basis the spirit of revolutionary change, and it is this mood that gives the four playwrights a commonality of interest and purpose. Ben Caldwell, for instance, shows his abomination of the Black who, because of ego and greed, will purposely deceive his own people or allow himself to be used as an instrument of oppression. This characteristic suggests that Caldwell has the same temperament and view toward the Black situation as Amiri Baraka. Caldwell also shows deference to Baraka for his dramatic style. Both playwrights utilize broad caricature and satire to moralize and condemn. Moreover, they both realize and appreciate the inherent ability of myth to dramatize conflicts and to simplify complicated theories. But Baraka is perhaps the more naturally gifted thinker and writer. He is by far the more original and intellectual, to say nothing of being more openly hostile and personally disillusioned. Caldwell's plays, often simplified to the point of caricature and old-fashioned melodrama, carry a plain and direct message.

On the other hand, Ron Milner and Ed Bullins share certain affinities of style and form. In *The Warning—A Theme for Linda*

Milner reflects a familiar Bullins proclivity for mixing presentational devices into an otherwise strictly representational play. In several instances reminiscent of Bullins' *Clara's Ole Man*, Milner's *The Warning* explores the experiences of Black youth facing the responsibilities of maturity. Both plays are sensitive to the peculiar problems Black youths face in trying to adapt sexual roles and morals to the realities of their oppressed condition. Milner and Bullins have chosen in each case to use a realistic mode bordering on naturalism. In his longer plays Bullins often mixes such devices as dream sequences and flashbacks with straight realism, a device Milner uses in *The Warning*. But the similarities between these two playwrights are not exemplified in their plays in *A Black Quartet*; with *The Gentleman Caller*, Bullins takes a stronger revolutionary posture for armed warfare, while Milner, with sensitivity and restraint, explores the meanings of Black womanhood and manhood. But the point to emphasize is that all four playwrights share a mood of revolt—both on the larger and the restricted scale—that threatened to revolutionize American society and the American theatre.

The Black Quartet, looked at not as separate plays by individual playwrights but as a single work with a defined ontology of its own, represents an alternative system of thought and action. In it aesthetics and politics unite for the purpose of changing the Black situation in America. In essence, *The Black Quartet* expresses an ideology commensurate with the philosophy of the Black Power Movement and the ideas of such Black Nationalist leaders as Malcolm X.

The purpose of the Black Theatre Movement as delineated through manifestoes, articles, and recognized spokesmen is twofold. First, the movement, a natural outgrowth of both the Civil Rights Movement and the Black Power Movement, shared their avowed objectives of fomenting rebellion against the suppression of the autonomous urge of Black people(s) to define and affirm concepts of existence, essence, and experience as they relate to the reality of being Black. "Black Theatre actually deals with the lives of Black people. It is a theatre that actually functions to liberate Black people," explained Baraka, a leading spokesman and functionary for the movement.[6] Second, functioning as a wing of the Black Arts Movement, the Black Theatre Movement also envisioned its special purpose to be the elevation of Black Consciousness on the one hand, and on the other the eradication of the negative Black image created by racist-oriented literature and media through the creation of a new, more positive Black image. It was Frantz Fanon, author of the influential works *The Wretched of the Earth* and *Black Skin, White Masks,* who pointed out that it was a negative self-image that caused Black people to feel insignificant and powerless to affect their environment and change their condition.[7] Literature and theatre could help to refute White claims and reeducate deluded Blacks. Carolyn F. Gerald, in "The Black Writer and His Role," warned, "We must reject white attempts at portraying Black reality."[8]

The conclusion reached through statements like that made by Gerald is that Black literature and drama have traditionally been evaluated by only one standard, the works of other White Western writers. Under such a standard, in order to get his work fairly judged and criticized, a Black writer had to emulate the style and reflect the values and point of view of White middle-class Americans. Those who continued to reflect a vision of truth and beauty that was diametrically opposed to what the dominant group wanted and needed to believe and feel, knew from the start they had chosen to be outcasts and had to create their own counter-system of literary values. Since the White critics represented the tastes and opinions of the majority group, this literary aesthetic was destined to be the clear-cut antithesis of the one being challenged. Black Arts critic and spokesman Larry Neal declared that the new Black Aesthetic would pose "a separate symbolism, mythology, critique, and iconology."[9]

Although the concept of a Black aesthetic first arose from the ranks of the "new" Black poets, it was based on the oral and musical (blues forms and Be-Bop) elements traditional to Black culture. Of course, other poets and writers, such as Langston Hughes, had incorporated these forms into their own works several decades before the poets of the 1960s. The Black poets of the 1960s, whether they were conscious of it or not, were merely continuing a trend toward the development of a Black aesthetic in literature that had begun as early as the 1920s. This apparent trend makes it difficult, and perhaps fruitless, to attempt to single out the individual who first called for a Black aesthetic; however, Larry Neal, in his essay "The Black Arts Movement," quotes poet Etheridge Knight as emphatically suggesting that "Unless the Black artist establishes a 'Black aesthetic' he will have no future at all."[10] The term obviously crystallized the philosophy of the Black Arts Movement.

Whoever started it notwithstanding, the major contributors to the rhetoric of the philosophy were Amiri Baraka and Ron Karenga. Karenga, one of the most militant and original theoreticians of the Black Power Movement, laid the groundwork for the creation of a new Black value system based on the rejection of all American values. As an alternative value system, it took into serious consideration the factors of economics, politics, socialization, lifestyle, frame of reference, and cultural expression as they related to Afro-Americans "colonized" within the United States. Baraka then synthesized the rhetoric of Black Power with that of Black Arts into a medium of expression. His vehicle, initially, was the poem. In the essay previously cited, Neal quotes a Baraka poem entitled "Black Art" to illustrate the underlying principle of the Black Arts philosophy—that Black Art is to be used as a means of effecting the physical, spiritual, psychological, and cultural liberation of Blacks:

> We want a black poem. And a
> Black World.
> Let the world be a Black Poem
> And Let All Black People Speak This Poem
> Silently
> Or LOUD[11]

For the Black artist, then, the traditional White aesthetic had become stagnant. It did not promote social causes or increase the moral awareness of those persons it proclaimed it served. It had, quite frankly, run its course. However, the Black Aesthetic was perceived outside narrow racial confines. If taken seriously by the society as a whole, its proponents believed it could pump new life into moribund cultural and social concepts. They saw the Black Aesthetic in the same dialectical terms described by Russian filmmaker Sergei Eisenstein, as:

The inception of new concepts and viewpoints in the conflict between customary conception and particular representation as dynamic—as a dynamization of the inertia of perception—as a dynamization of the "traditional view" into a new one.[12]

Advocates of the Black Aesthetic naturally inveighed against the Western view of art as something separate from everyday life. The concept of art-for-art's-sake was anathema to the Black Aesthetic, which placed heavy stress on the functional meaning of art. The Black Aesthetic was, most of all, about change, but in order to make an impact on a substantial segment of American society, the Black Arts Movement had first to engender change within the ranks of Afro-Americans themselves. Because the credo of the Black Arts Movement also stressed commitment to the liberation of Black people, it was committed to the broader idea of human rights. Basically, Black Art advocated the use of artistic and creative means to achieve political ends.

Since the Black Aesthetic focused sharply on elevating and developing individual and collective consciousness, obviously its primary methodologies were persuasion and didacticism. From the beginning, attempts were made by certain critics and reviewers to subcategorize the Black Arts Movement under the banner of the social consciousness of the 1930s. The Black Arts Movement, however, emphatically denied any interest in "protest" literature or drama. Protest literature implies that "subordinates" are supplicating "superiors" to undergo a moral appraisal. In short, protest is appealing to the "enemy." Protest is what characterized the majority of Black literature and drama prior to the beginning of the 1960s. Black Art was not about winning the hearts and minds of White people; rather, it was about revolt and revolution. The problem it confronted was caused by conflict, so as a tactical device Black Art encouraged aggravation of the conflict, realizing that it is certainly the nature of conflict ultimately to work its way out through violence (revolution), compromise, or evolution.

The dominant rhetoric adopted by the Black Arts Movement was that of revolution but the use of the term sometimes caused confusion. *Revolution* is defined in dictionary terms as "a forcible overthrow of an established government or political system by the people governed." However, a second definition from the same source is "a complete, pervasive, usually radical change in something, often one made relatively quickly."[13] When advocates of either the Black Power Movement or the Black Arts Movement used the term *revolution*, it sometimes had to be qualified. For example, Karenga could write in 1967, "The revolution being fought now is a revolution to win the minds of Black people."[14] Therefore, the revolutionary ideology of the Black Aesthetic was more than mere protest or political reform. In addition to serving as a means of effecting political and social change, it aspired to the more monumental and idealistic task of affecting the masses of Black people with a new sense of identity and spiritualism. Although somewhat fragmentary and inconclusive, the components of the Black Aesthetic can be broken down into the following broad categories: (1) political, (2) ontological, and (3) cultural (artistic/creative).

From a political standpoint, the Black Aesthetic tried to address itself to the material and social needs of Black people. To achieve these goals, a reorientation was necessary to rehabilitate the majority of Blacks, who had been brainwashed and psychologically maimed by centuries of physical and mental abuse. The American system was charged with having institutionalized policies and practices demeaning the image of African-Americans, while also diminishing and distorting their individual and collective contributions and overall significance to American society. The average Black person had no frame of reference, no means of perceiving himself as a unique individual, other than through the eyes of a majority group. The Black man's concept of himself was not based on his consciousness but was instead a secondhand view. Having to define himself through a surrogate consciousness, the Black person was shut off from direct contact with universal reality and his own sense of being. Certainly, this situation suggests a kind of mental and spiritual imprisonment, so the early proponents of the Black Aesthetic concluded that what most Blacks needed was a revolution of consciousness.

Ontologically, the movement called for a radical concept of self, freedom, and responsibility. The result was to be the development of a more self-conscious and more self-confident individual, one sensitive and fully cognizant of the world and his or her place in determining its destiny.

Culturally speaking, the Black Aesthetic had two purposes. First, it would synthesize and codify all those creative and artistic expressions peculiar to Afro-Americans into one well-defined aesthetic. If it were to fashion this new aesthetic out of the matrix of the Black culture that already existed, the Black Aesthetic naturally needed to concentrate on those cultural elements obviously indigenous to Afro-Americans—Black religion, gospel music and classical spirituals, dance, jazz, and the blues. Beyond these creative and artistic elements of the culture, the aesthetic also sought to include those unique aspects of Black life such as Black rhetoric, with its particular style of diction and syntax, street styles (such as dress and expressions), and kinesics (such as walking, mannerisms, and expressions). The second cultural function of the Black Aesthetic was to set up a criterion for the analysis and evaluation, on ethical and artistic grounds, of works created by Afro-Americans and others committed to the concepts of Black self-determination and Black Art.

The most original and innovative ideas have come from the playwrights among the Black Arts group, and as it stands, the two playwrights who have dominated this group are Amiri Baraka and Ed Bullins. Both writers have made outstanding contributions to the movement in terms of plays and theories. Although Bullins admits to being influenced by Baraka early in his playwriting career, Bullins more than Baraka clarified techniques of Black dramaturgy. Baraka, perhaps the more intellectual and original artist, tends to be somewhat philosophical and visionary as a dramatic theorist. He has been more successful in demonstrating his ideas through his plays than in exploring them in his theoretical writings. Baraka strongly espoused the concept of "Revolutionary Theatre" as an alternative to the conventional type of Black Theatre, but much of the remainder of the theory depends on Antonin Artaud for its substance. "This should be a theatre of World Spirit," Baraka wrote, "where the spirit can be shown to be the most competent force in the world. Force. Spirit. Feeling."[15] Again reflecting Artaud, Baraka conceives of theatre as a means of changing the essential nature of human beings.[16] Of course, where Artaud proposes to accomplish this feat through alchemy, Baraka chooses violence to effect his changes. Furthermore, Baraka and Artaud agree on the issue that theatre should be a collective experience of purification. Artaud evidently had an impact on Bullins too, who agrees with the French theorist's view that the theatre must destroy all corrupt customs, morals, and values before a new awakening can be achieved by everyone witnessing the play.

Differences are apparent between Baraka and Artaud. For example, Baraka takes the use of violence literally, whereas Artaud distinguished between the meaning inherent within the act and the act itself. Artaud called his theatre a theatre of cruelty, but he intended that the concept should not be confused with physical abuse or assault on individuals. Thus, cruelty depicted on Artaud's stage was suggestive and emotional, with no apparent attempts to portray actors inflicting violence on each other. Baraka's plays, on the other hand, vividly depict violent acts being committed by individuals against other individuals. His advocacy of violence as a literary device rests on the view that violence can be used as a means of discovering and shaping one's identity, a view that is in keeping with the ways in which violence has been used in such recognized masterpieces as *Macbeth*, *Moby Dick*, and *Crime and Punishment*. In these works violence is depicted as a positive, creative act, establishing or affirming the individual's position and destiny within the universe.

As a dramatic technique, Baraka uses violence therapeutically. In other words, just as a surgeon must "cut out" the sickness (itself a form of violence) from the patient's body, the Black playwright, in Baraka's view, must use violence to counteract the violence that has been done to the Black image and to Black minds. In *Dutchman* Baraka goes so far as to suggest that the collective Black neurosis is the result of centuries of scorn and degradation and that the cure for it is for Blacks to kill White people. This reference to ritualized therapy comes across more as a literary conceit than a practical prescription, however. Another variation on the violence theme in Baraka's *Madheart* is a dramatized exorcism, an attempt to drive out the "devil-demon" that controls the minds and bodies of Black men and women. And in his more community-conscious plays, such as *Experimental Death Unit #1* and *Junkies Are Full of (Shhh . . .)*, Baraka uses violence as a counterforce to purge the Black community of those who by their very nature are harbingers of violence and corruption.

Artaud was attracted to the music and splendor of the oriental theatre. Those ingredients, he insisted, were lacking from the mundane theatre of the West, with its emphasis on surface realism, speech, and psychological conflict. Music was also important to Baraka, who attributed to Black music the power to invigorate and revitalize a listless American theatre. Baraka's keen interest in Black music resulted in the writing of two knowledgeable and significant works. Baraka's admiration for certain contemporary jazz musicians inspired him to emphasize within many of his dramatic works the Black man's musical heritage. In many ways, the music of avant-garde musician-composer Sun-Ra seems to have had much influence on the creation of *Black Mass*, for example, as did the myth of Yakub. Sun-Ra and his Myth-Science Arkestra, who performed the background music for the original production, are also heard on the recorded version of the play. It is also interesting, in view of *Black Mass'* flamboyant mix of carnival and space-opera, that Sun-Ra claims to have actually traveled to various distant planets in quest of "interplanetary music" and "interplanetary intelligence." Baraka comes closest to realizing a dramatic style structured like a musical composition in *Slaveship*, a play in two parts and three movements.

Music is also integral to Ed Bullins' plays, especially those within the Twentieth Century Cycle—an ambitious undertaking that will eventually include twenty plays that explore the experiences and trace the lives of a select cast of characters. Unlike Baraka, who insists on original, improvised scores integrated into the mise-en-scène, Bullins settles for popular recordings of the period. He seems, therefore, to seek an authenticity that only pure realism can achieve. In fact, quite early in his career, Bullins spoke out in favor of a "theatre of reality" that personifies honesty and integrity. However, in his own proposed theatre of reality, and in subsequent plays such as *In*

the Wine Time, Going' a Buffalo, and *The Duplex,* he seems to es-
chew the quasi-scientific methodology inherent in traditional
naturalism. Designed to be more inductive than deductive, his
approach is not to draw preconceived conclusions and then
proceed to explain and justify them. Obviously, Bullins never
intended to write the well-made play. In explaining what he
meant by a theatre of reality, Bullins wrote:

The revolutionary nature of this theatre is not of style and technique
but of theme and character. . . . So it is not a call for [sic] a return to
realism or naturalism that this theatre calls for [sic]: it is the exposure
of illusion through exploding myths and lies that are disguised as reality and truths.[17]

Bullins' technique was to allow his characters to tell their own
stories, revealing to each other and to the audience only what
they want to. Bullins never takes sides or imposes his own personal point of view upon the action. Everything is very "natural," though obviously not naturalistic. It is as if Bullins were
projecting onto the stage images of real-life people and/or types
that he has met or known, using the inner eye of his memory
like the lens of a movie camera. Still this particular style is
somewhat in keeping with the special needs and requirements
of a distinct Black Aesthetic, for during the 1960s heavy emphasis was placed on Black "naturalness." Bullins argues that
the nature of the Black Experience demands unadulterated
reality, and he further contends that since Whites are afraid of
reality, their writers and artists try to avoid a confrontation with
it.[18] Simply, the hypothesis was that since the experiences of
Blacks were natural dramatic events in themselves, full of iron-
ies, complications, conflicts, and insurmountable obstacles, they
need only to be packaged for the stage as is. "Imitation of an
action," as posited by Aristotle, came to mean something done
secondhand, the author and actors being removed from the actual experience and so utilizing a strictly objective perspective.
To the supporters of this "natural school," the dramatic event
meant Black actors being themselves in real-life situations. Art
and life were allowed to merge and become as one.

Theodore Hudson in his book *From LeRoi Jones to Amiri Bar-*

aka chose the term *impromptu theatre* to describe those plays of Baraka's that tend to espouse direct revolutionary involvement, but it somehow seems inaccurate to categorize this form of Street Theatre as impromptu. *Extemporaneous theatre* is more appropriate, since these particular plays are based on improvisations or variations on a single theme. Besides, in practically all cases the playwright prepared a complete script for the play. Nothing, therefore, was ever completely spontaneous or impromptu. Though scripted, the play nevertheless depends heavily on pantomime and nonverbal expression—in other words, improvised action that communicates a specific message. However, it was Bullins, not Baraka, who outlined the criteria for Street Theatre:

Street Theatre is the name given to the play or dramatic piece (i.e., skit, morality or political fare or black commercial that subliminally broadcasts blackness) written expressly to be presented upon the urban streets or adapted to that purpose. . . . The plays should be short, sharp, incisive. Contemporary themes, satirical pieces on current counterrevolutionary figures or enemies of the people, humorous themes, also children's plays with revolutionary lessons are good street play material. Also startling, unique material, something that gives the masses identifying images, symbols and challenging situations.[19]

Both Baraka and Bullins held that content and subject matter should be central to the composition of a play, while style and form should be secondary. In addition, they perceived literature to be of sociological import. This viewpoint reflects a basic Marxist philosophy of literature, but the kind of theatre advocated by Bullins and Baraka should not be misconstrued as simplistic protest drama: No appeals are being made to the White majority. Rather, the purpose of what Bullins refers to as Black Revolutionary Agit-Prop is to create a line of:

communication with diverse classes of people, the Black working class, or with special groups (e.g., winos, pool hall brothers, prostitutes, pimps, hypes, etc.), who would not ordinarily come or be drawn into the theatre.[20]

Harold Cruse alleged that the various Black Theatre groups failed to develop a body of criticism.[21] Perhaps even lower on their list of priorities was serious audience analysis, particularly relating to the Black audience. As it turned out, audience analysis was taken up primarily by writers and critics working within the area of educational theatre. During the 1968 summer institute in repertory theatre, participated in largely by students and teachers from predominantly Black high schools and colleges, a major complaint of both students and teachers concerned the general lack of sophistication on the part of the average Black audience. Of course, these references were to audiences who attended plays produced by high schools and colleges; still, as William Reardon and Thomas Pawley point out in their book, *The Black Theatre and the Dramatic Arts*, if a Black person does not learn to appreciate and to relate to the theatrical experience within the educational setting, where is he likely to learn?[22] The majority of Black Theatre artists themselves are products of colleges, universities, and dramatic schools. A trained audience seems a prerequisite to the creation of what Baraka envisioned when he established the Harlem Black Arts Theatre—a truly independent Black Theatre. It has to be remembered that aesthetics do include "principles of taste." Implied within any system of aesthetics is a certain set of established rules of etiquette and decorum. The question is: If the development of a Black audience was desirable and necessary, then why was not every attempt made to first prepare the audience? This way, it seems, an aesthetic criterion could grow out of the collective ethos of the people themselves. Perhaps the groups overemphasized the audience's adaptation to the artists, rather than the artists' adaptation to the audience.

Nonetheless, Thomas Pawley made some interesting observations regarding the unique character and personality of the typical Black audience in the August–September 1971 issue of *Players* under the title "The Black Theatre Audience." Pawley's views, while unsupported by scientific research, are the result of years of serious observation. Although he concentrates his attention primarily upon the behavior of the Black college audience, experience has shown that many of these same reactions are displayed by Black audiences within the commercial theatre setting. According to Pawley:

With efforts being made to build Black Theatre and . . . the increasing demand by students for Black Theatre on college campuses, it might be well to describe this student behavior more specifically, to analyze its causes and to suggest ways of controlling it without destroying its spontaneous exuberance and enthusiasm.[23]

Pawley also makes it clear that the peculiar habits displayed by members of the typical Black audience do not set them apart as abnormal; these traits may be atypical only when compared to those behavior patterns of a specific White middle-class audience.

Members of the typical Black audience, Pawley concludes, tend to react both verbally and nonverbally, to express their reactions and emotions by clapping their hands, stomping their feet, and verbally addressing the actors on stage. Their reaction is the result of a special kind of cultural conditioning resulting from experiences in the church service, the nightclub stage show, and sports events. A characteristic of the traditional Black Church has always been the free, spontaneous expression of emotions. In fact, verbal responses from members of the congregation are not only expected but encouraged. Pawley notes that a Black Baptist minister, for example, is likely to be chagrined if his sermon does not arouse spirited outbursts. In *Blues People* Baraka points out that this peculiar cultural trait is based on the "call-and-response" pattern of traditional African and slave work songs.[24] Even nightclub entertainers usually encourage their audiences to sing and clap. The sports crowd cheers what pleases and satisfies and boos what displeases and disappoints, and this behavior carries over into the theatre experience. Of course, Black people are not the only ones who frequent nightclubs and attend sports events; but behavior patterns conditioned by these sources are likely to be evident in the Black person's theatrical response since his exposure to the traditional patterns of behavior found in the theatre is limited. Architects of the Black Aesthetic were eager to tap precisely these cultural sources (with the exception of the reaction of sports crowds). Scenes depicting a Black Church service appear in James Baldwin's *The Amen Corner* and *Blues for Mister Charlie*. *The Sty of the Blind Pig* and

The First Breeze of Summer utilize the Black Church service, and Ed Bullins uses gospel music recordings in his play *In the Wine Time*. Barbara Ann Teer's Harlem National Black Theatre developed the concept of "God-conscious" art to replace European "self-centered" art, which she believed to be conditioned by materialism and based on external feeling. God-conscious art, on the other hand, was supposedly guided by the creative impulses that emanate from within.

Whether or not the Black Theatre Movement can take credit, more and more Blacks are attending live theatre today. To take advantage of this new market, Broadway producers have especially exploited the Black musical. Even though few of these musicals qualify as original Black creations, Blacks have regularly attended in record numbers. Not restricted to New York City, this trend has reappeared wherever road companies have taken these musicals once they have been successful in New York. The implication, therefore, is that the mass Black audience, like the mass White audience, prefers musicals and comedy on the whole to the more serious and cerebral plays. But the fact that community theatres—with a few exceptions, most of them scions of the Black Theatre Movement—are still active in many parts of the country means that some audiences support a more committed theatre. Many observers believe that what Black interest is being shown in community theatre productions is mostly a by-product of the interest stimulated by the bigger, more commercial shows. However, reporting on the success of NEC in building a significant following, Douglas Turner Ward says, "When we started out we got audiences that were about 80 per cent white. Now that situation has just about reversed itself."[25] Ward readily admits that the plays that have achieved the most success with Black audiences are those that have been naturalistic portrayals of Black family life. Incidentally, Ward sees this as a trend that might be continued. The Black writer, he feels, is experiencing a desire to explore his own background using the medium of naturalism. He sees this as synonymous with what Sean O'Casey did with the Irish experience. He also feels that there is often alienation between White writers and their audience, whereas the Black writer and the Black audience share a closer relationship.[26]

From all indications, the Black interest in legitimate theatre is the result of conditioning by other entertainment media. The musical, of course, can be enjoyed by everyone because of its escapist value, but television and the movies have no doubt contributed considerably to Black interest in the theatre. For example, the simulated "live" theatre format used by Norman Lear for "Sanford and Son," "Good Times," and "The Jeffersons" must have certainly won converts to this particular style of presentation. Moreover, television productions such as the adaptations of Ernest Gaines' *The Autiobiography of Miss Jane Pittman* and Alex Haley's *Roots* surely aroused a demand for more conscientious treatment of the Black Experience. And, too, the Black films of the late 1960s and early 1970s, whatever their inherent quality and value, merely whetted the appetites of Black audiences for more entertainment in which the Black man/woman triumphs against heavy odds and emerges a hero. An example of a play that capitalized on this interest in melodrama was Ron Milner's *What the Wine-Sellers Buy.* Nonetheless, Blacks are indeed attending more live theatre than ever before, but it is doubtful that this means there is a cohesive, viable Black audience. The Black Theatre Movement, while surely a factor in developing Black interest in legitimate theatre, has been only partly successful in making the appreciation of Black Theatre, not to mention the Black Arts per se, and any attending system of Black aesthetics, part of the cultural ethos of American Blacks.

NOTES

1. Jean Genet, *The Blacks: A Clown Show* (New York: Grove Press, 1960).
2. Thomas D. Pawley, "The First Black Playwrights," *Black World* 21 (April 1972): 16.
3. Loften Mitchell, *Black Drama* (New York: Hawthorn Books, 1967), p. 88.
4. Stuart W. Little, *Off-Broadway: The Prophetic Theatre* (New York: Coward, McCann and Geoghegan, 1972), p. 100.
5. Clayton Riley, ed., Introduction to *A Black Quartet* (New York: New American Library/A Mentor Book, 1970), p. vii.
6. Michael Coleman, "What Is Black Theatre? An Interview with Imamu Amiri Baraka," *Black World* 20 (April 1971):32–36.

7. Frantz Fanon, *Black Skin, White Masks* (New York: Grove Press/Evergreen Black Cat Edition, 1978), p. 110.

8. Carolyn F. Gerald, "The Black Writer and His Role," in *The Black Aesthetic*, ed. Addison Gayle, Jr. (New York: Doubleday,/Anchor Books, 1972), p. 354.

9. Larry Neal, "The Black Arts Movement," *Tulane Drama Review* 12 (Summer 1968): 29.

10. Ibid., p. 30.

11. Ibid., p. 32.

12. Sergei Eisenstein, *Film Form* (New York: Harcourt, Brace and World/A Harvest Book, 1949), p. 47.

13. *The Random House College Dictionary*, rev. ed. (1969), s.v. "revolution."

14. Maulana Ron Karenga, "From the Quotable Karenga," in *The Black Power Revolt: A Collection of Essays*, ed. Floyd B. Barbour (New York: Collier Books, 1968), p. 125.

15. Amiri Baraka, "In Search of the Revolutionary Theatre," *Black World* 15 (April 1966): 22.

16. Antonin Artaud, *The Theatre and Its Double* (New York: Grove Press, 1958), pp. 15–31.

17. Ed Bullins, "Theatre of Reality," *Black World* 15 (April 1966): 65.

18. Ed Bullins, "The So-Called Western Avant-Garde Drama," in *Black Expression: Essays by and about Black Americans in the Creative Arts*, ed. Addison Gayle, Jr. (New York: Weybright and Talley, 1969), p. 145.

19. Ed Bullins, "On Street Theatre," *Tulane Drama Review* 12 (Summer 1968): 93.

20. Ibid.

21. Harold Cruse, *The Crisis of the Negro Intellectual* (New York: William Morrow and Co., 1967), pp. 540–42.

22. William R. Reardon and Thomas D. Pawley, *The Black Theatre and the Dramatic Arts: A Dialogue, Bibliography, and Anthology* (Westport, Conn.: Negro Universities Press, 1970).

23. Thomas D. Pawley, "The Black Theatre Audience," *Players* (August–September 1971): 258.

24. LeRoi Jones, *Blues People* (New York: William Morrow and Co., 1963), p. 62.

25. Elenor Lester, " 'We Exist to Create a Real Black Theatre': Seasons with the Negro Ensemble Company," *New York Times*, 2 March 1975, sec. 2, p. 5.

26. Ibid.

2

Blackness: A Dialectic of Experience

Whatever dramaturgy the playwrights of the Black Theatre Movement chose to utilize, invariably the frame of reference that distinguished their plays from others was based on their concepts of the Black Experience or Black Consciousness—or both. There can be a Black Experience without Black Consciousness, but there can be no Black Consciousness without the Black Experience. Closely related but not exactly synonymous, the Black Experience is a definition (or a condition) of existence, while Black Consciousness is a condition of both existence and essence. Existence comprehends phenomena that can be explained scientifically, but essence is noumenal and is only accessible through discursive, metaphoric language. Existence is a fact; essence is a possibility. Of course, once defined, essence becomes a quality. And within time, and with the power to enforce it, this quality too can be transformed into a quantity, thence into a fact. Existence establishes the fact that something actually *is* while essence establishes exactly *what* that something is.

In the long debate between traditional philosophy and the modern philosophies such as Existentialism and Marxism, essence is given priority over existence in the view of the traditionalists. Therefore, in the traditional view, even before man begins to exist, his essence has already been predetermined by some higher power or god. On the other hand, Existentialism and Marxism see man as already existent and constantly striving for freedom and perfection. From this point of view, essence, as it relates to human beings, is not predetermined, but mutable within the context of changing historical events. Human beings have the prerogative, therefore, to define their essence, to create their own values, and to set goals for themselves; all men, regardless of race or ethnicity, have this prerogative. The Black Consciousness Movement of the 1960s was an assertion of Black self-determination and Black identity, qualities long denied Blacks in a traditionally anti-Black society.

Black Consciousness is the result of alienation between two groups, or races, of individuals that find themselves locked in a conflict of wills. Black Consciousness is a product of conflict, a conflict that mainly has to do with sharp disagreement over what constitutes reality and the conditions for individual freedom. The attempt by Western Whites to impose a system of thinking and acting onto Blacks has created conditions necessitating the militant development of a Black Consciousness. However, one must remember that Existentialism and Marxism, as well as the traditional philosophies that preceded them, are primarily European in origin. And it is understood that philosophies, like mythologies, are originated by and oriented toward specific cultures.

Psychiatrist and social revolutionary–philosopher Frantz Fanon states in *Black Skin, White Masks,* "Ontology—once it is finally admitted as leaving existence by the wayside—does not permit us to understand the being of the Black man."[1] Although the statement itself sounds somewhat ambiguous, the obvious attempt is to discredit ontology as primarily the creation of literary minds. The Existentialist philosopher Martin Heidegger is quoted as claiming, "It is in words and language that things first come into being and are."[2] This statement further supports the idea that a language of some kind must precede any concept of being. Ontologies are language-bound and can only be comprehended in terms of the language out of which they were originated. Notes psychologist Julian Jaynes:

When we talk about what goes on in the mind-space, we use metaphors taken from physical behavior in actual space. . . . Just as the words we use to describe what goes on in consciousness are metaphors, so the mind-space in which these functions take place is likewise metaphorical.[3]

Anthropologist Richard Leakey theorizes that shared consciousness among humans is possible because they are able through language to describe inner feelings and mental images.[4] For instance, *muntu* in traditional Bantu philosophy is a word-concept that signifies "human being." In that same language, *kintu* refers to inanimate objects, while *hantu* designates the idea of time and place; moreover, *Kuntu* means form, structure, or logic.[5] Definitely, there are as many languages as there are races, ethnic groups, and tribal societies, each ascribing to the symbols contained within its language system. All human beings, nevertheless, seem to share an awareness of time, place, and the sensation of existence. Essence, therefore, because it is so subjective and based on value judgments, is primarily descriptive and literary. In other words, the essence of a thing can only be described in symbolic and visual terms, and the act of describing is itself a literary device. Fanon's conclusion, then, seems to rest on the premise that *ontology* too is a literary term, perhaps coined by metaphysicians as a means of explaining the phenomenon of existence. In this Platonic sense, existence becomes just as much a product of the creative (intuitive) mind as it is a product of nature.

Fanon appears further to suggest that existence, the recognizable presence of solid matter, can exist as is, without being described and classified. Thus, the suggestion seems to include the belief that existence is independent of literary description and definition. More importantly, any methodology can be disastrous when the group that conceives it also believes it to be the only universal method of defining existence. The unpleasant result is that the dominant group refuses to recognize any other system(s) that might be equally valid, with its own inherent strengths. Thus, the historical basis for the racial conflict encountered between descendants and inhabitants of Europe and those of Africa seems to be the result of two distinct systems of knowledge—one literate and the other primarily oral. The European literary tradition formulated and canonized the concepts of existence and essence through historical, philosophical, and literary chronicles. On the other hand, African oral tradition formulated and passed down the concepts of existence and essence through poems, songs, music, and oral history. The Black man's concepts of his own being and essence have been overshadowed by the dominating powers of recorded literature and history.

Both Existentialism and Marxism purport to go beyond group and racial boundaries by emphasizing a concern for the conditions of life as they affect *all* men, yet the two philosophies conflict with each other through diametrically opposed attitudes and approaches to the human condition. Existentialism takes a subjective attitude toward life in the belief that individual consciousness gives form and substance to reality. This view holds that without the existence of the human factor—man's mind and his awareness—the universe would probably not exist. Consequently, man's purpose is absurd. He must verify the existence of a universe he can neither fully comprehend nor control.

On the other hand, Marxism takes a strictly objective attitude toward life, reducing the importance of the human factor in verifying the universe's existence. Furthermore, instead of taking a pessimistic view toward life, Marxists conclude from the obvious historical development of the human species that there is a sense to life. The Marxist also believes that in science, man has at his disposal the means to comprehend and to control nature. Finally, instead of viewing the individual in conflict with his environment as the Existentialist does, the Marxist perceives a symbiotic relationship between the two.

The conflict between the two dominant ideologies of modern times is sharpest over individual freedom. Some Existentialists feel the only choice the individual has is to strive in despair. Other Existentialist writers, such as Albert Camus, believe the individual can experience the sensation of freedom by rebelling vigorously against those forces of the universe that threaten to destroy him. For the Marxist, individual freedom is gained not by declaring war on the universe, but by reducing its forces to scientific principles and making them useful. Further, the control and regulation of social institutions so they are made to provide the maximum liberties for all individuals rather than for a few to the exclusion of others, is germane to Marxist thought.

A study of the Black situation in modern history presents a

clear picture of the problems and contradictions that both Existentialism and Marxism attempt to confront. Curiously, the fact that Black people exist in the world in the same form and substance as do all other people has perplexed colonizers and subjugators. The European press to expand territorially and economically first brought them into contact with races of darker skin, and the European consciousness shaped and guided by its systems of mythology that elaborately structured into hierarchies all humanlike races and classes—stimulated the European expansionists to live out their primal fantasies when they met humans they perceived as backward or inferior to themselves. Understandably, if not logically, the undeveloped consciousness of these Europeans caused them to simplify a real world which had suddenly become contradictory and confusing by falling back on the ordered world of mythology. Interestingly, this concept can be read into James Baldwin's *Blues for Mister Charlie*. In this work Baldwin perceives the American system of stratification as having many features in common with ancient canons of mythology. In effect, man throughout the ages has found it necessary to devise means to explain and justify his existence and essence within the universe. Therefore, in cases where only one race rules supreme, completely unchallenged by rival groups, stratification is based on an elaborate religious mythology (gods, demigods, mortals, etc.). But where the opposite situation exists, racial or class stratification will serve the same purpose. Baldwin seems to infer that in the United States a racial system as well as a religious mythology exists. Furthermore, both of these systems have been distorted and corrupted to such an extent that they have caused an erosion of human dignity rather than the elevation of it. Consequently, it is these kinds of conditions that have made the Black Experience possible.

Life under the domination of archetypes that are not really an integral part of his own consciousness has been the most profound mode of slavery the Black man has encountered in a society whose dominant group was able to perpetuate the heritage of its own mythology. Thus, the Black man has had to develop a "double consciousness," for he not only has had to think as a Black person, but he also has had to be able to comprehend the same reality as those who had the power to define the world in which he existed. Locked into such an ironclad caste system, the Black man found it almost impossible to conceive of himself as an individual. His expression of individual freedom, free will, could take only one form, rebellion. For this reason, philosophers such as Sartre, Genet, and members of the Beat Generation saw within the Black person the perfect Existential being. Black Consciousness eventually meant accepting a Black identity rather than transcending it. Black Consciousness allows the Black person to be "Black" both as a member of a collective and as an individual.

Black people have a natural affinity for the spoken word. For the majority of Blacks, then, literature is an elitist pastime. It is also, in the European tradition, anti-Black. The intention of reaching the Black masses prompted the artists within the Black Arts Movement to use poetry—poetry intended to be read aloud—as their main medium of expression, but plays too were perceived as having equal potential for effectiveness. "Plays reach our people better than literature or books," Baraka wrote in a paper entitled "Black Revolutionary Poets Should Also Be Playwrights."[6] Therefore, the effectiveness of the Black playwright should be judged by a system of criticism that takes the spoken word into account. Black dramatists must be evaluated according to their ability to transform the Black oral tradition into the medium of art and thereby contribute to the development of positive consciousness in their audience.

NOTES

1. Frantz Fanon, *Black Skin, White Masks* (New York: Grove Press/Evergreen Black Cat Edition, 1978), p. 110.

2. George Novack, ed., *Existentialism Versus Marxism: Conflicting Views on Humanism* (New York: Dell Publishing Co./A Delta Book, 1966), p. 325.

3. Julian Jaynes, "The Lost Voices of Gods: Reflections on the Dawn of Consciousness," *Psychology Today* 11 (November 1977): 60.

4. Richard Leakey, "Origins of the Mind," *Psychology Today* 12 (July 1978): 54.

5. Janheinz Jahn, *Muntu: An Outline of the New African Culture* (New York: Grove Press, 1961), p. 100.

6. Amiri Baraka, "Black Revolutionary Poets Should Also Be Playwrights," *Black World* 21 (April 1972): 5.

3

Identity and Survival: Black Theatre Companies during the Movement

In 1965 the Black Theatre Movement was launched onto a course of revolutionary and community-based theatre. Four years later the collective nature of this new movement was publicly proclaimed through the production of four one-act plays under the title *A Black Quartet*. In the year 1971 another significant event occurred when the Black Theatre Alliance (BTA) was officially incorporated. The creation of this alliance was an answer to those critics who dismissed as fantasy the idea that a Black Theatre existed. Formation of the alliance was a natural reaction by individual theatre companies to the need to survive financially. But just as important was the need for these groups to secure services that would enhance their artistic development and refine their ability to reach larger audiences by publicizing themselves and their productions. Consequently, the idea to form a Black theatre alliance was conceived by members of small, commercially anonymous community groups whose biggest problem was raising funds. Mutual interest in survival, therefore, inspired Delano Stewart of the Bed-Stuy Theatre, Hazel Bryant of the Afro-American Total Theatre, and Roger Furman of the New Heritage Repertory Theatre Company to organize the Black Theatre Alliance. Delano Stewart had proposed the idea of the alliance and was BTA's first president; Hazel Bryant was secretary, and Ernie McClintock of the Afro-American Studio for Acting and Speech was BTA's vice president. Other founding officers were Roger Furman as executive secretary and

Cecil Cummings of the Brownsville Laboratory Theatre as treasurer. Initially BTA was composed of seven companies that were original members. These companies were the Afro-American Singing Theatre, the Afro-American Studio for Acting and Speech, Afro-American Total Theatre, Bed-Stuy Theatre, Brownsville Laboratory Theatre, New Heritage Repertory Theatre, and Theatre Black. Besides raising funds and providing technical and administrative services, the Black Theatre Alliance wanted to convince the public that Black Theatre was more than a passing fad.

As it was, important funding agencies refused to fund companies that were judged to be artistically substandard, thus BTA's concern with acquiring adequate lighting equipment, sets, and other technical facilities was due to both a desire and a need to improve the quality of member companies. And not only were fledgling Black theatre companies hampered by inadequate facilities and often inferior equipment, they also lacked administrative expertise needed to secure funding from public and private agencies. Moreover, while many avant-garde theatre companies could afford the luxury of experimentation for its own sake, Black theatres had to prove their worth to the community. Therefore, in November 1972, with a grant from the New York City Parks, Recreation and Cultural Affairs Administration, BTA sponsored a promotional theatre festival. Concomitantly, the alliance secured as executive director Joan Sandler, an administrator for the same New York City Parks, Recreation and Cultural Affairs Administration. When Sandler took over she observed, "At a time when established entrepreneurs, such as Joe Papp, are undercutting Black Theatre groups financially with their 'recognized' Black theatre projects and programs, Blacks with the same expertise in the same areas of interest are ignored by the funding organizations in preference for whites."[1] Sandler concluded that if Black Theatre was to survive in the United States, this dilemma had to be resolved, so to better read the business indicators of the theatre industry, she moved the BTA offices to 1564 Broadway. Because the office had been housed in the quarters used by the Afro-American Studio for Acting and Speech at 415 West 127 Street, the move farther downtown was opposed by some BTA members who felt the offices should remain in the Black community. However, this brief disagreement was quickly settled, and all agreed that the Broadway location would be politically advantageous.

Two years after its formation, the alliance produced the first issue of its newsletter, *Black Theatre Alliance*. In this newsletter the organization delineated its purposes and goals and declared itself "as a collective to solve common problems, to share information and resources and to create an instrument to validate Black Theatres as community institutions."[2] More specific goals included the development of a wider audience base, the establishment of a clearinghouse for information related to the theatre, the implementation of new funding sources and new programs, the promotion of member companies, and the provision of low-cost graphics and technical equipment. Also included was a provision that provided touring assistance and information. At the time the first newsletter was published, there were sixteen member companies, all based in the New York City area. The new members were the Cornbread Players, the New Federal Theatre, Black Vibrations, the Demi-Gods, the Urban Arts Corps, Weusi Kuunba Troupe, the East River Players, the New Lafayette Theatre, and Voices, Inc.

Through an alignment with the Theatre Communications Group (TCG), BTA was helped in the achievement of its goals and objectives. TCG provided all of the following: information on casting and touring, announcements of student auditions, visitation and personnel programs, subscription consultation, files on directors and theatre resources, publications, a theatre reference book, and access to a Black Theatre panel. A joint venture between BTA and TCG resulted in the compilation and issuance of the *Black Theatre Resources Directory*. National in scope, the directory listed Black Theatre directors, Black community theatre groups, works by Black playwrights, and the names of technicians and administrators.

In a way, the Black Theatre Movement of the 1960s and 1970s was a theatre in search of an audience. While the playwrights and plays emerged and community theatres proliferated, there was no sizable audience waiting eagerly in the wings. Roger Furman summed up the dilemma faced by Black Theatre companies by stating frankly:

I have yet to see Black Theatre have lines around it. . . . We have no choice but to do theatre for the people and my only plight is how to get the people into the theatre . . . its just a handful of people and there's not enough Black Panthers or radicals to break the box office.[3]

It was a serious concern, for if enough Black people did not support Black Theatre, then it could never become independent. It would inevitably remain dependent upon White-controlled foundations and philanthropy and never realize itself as a monolithic ethnic institution. Black Theatre artists seemed trapped in a paradox wherein the very people they were trying to bring into the theatre were those whose lifestyles they often scrutinized and ridiculed. Like Furman, Hazel Bryant expressed dismay: "One of the problems of Black Theatre is that we have kept it geared to a certain kind of experience—junkies, a lot about prostitutes. The grass roots didn't want to come and see plays about winos and junkies and prostitutes, because they live in it."[4] Moreover, the Black middle-class usually came under harsh criticism and vituperative attack. Of course, in most cases the strategy was to shock and outrage the audience into changing their way of thinking and living. Still, a serious communication problem existed in the Black community between Black Theatre artists and the denizens. Furman and Bryant were key founders of BTA and were genuinely concerned enough to seek a solution.

Since audience development was recognized as such a crucial factor, BTA sought expertise in this area. Vivian Robinson, president of the Audience Development Committee (Audelco), was contacted to help BTA in the implementation of audience development and communications. Although Audelco was founded as an independent service and support organization, it and the Black Theatre Alliance shared the same goals and mission. Formed in 1973 as a voluntary organization, Audelco's stated objective was the creation of new audiences as a means of stimulating an interest in and appreciation of the arts in Black communities.[5] As a non-profit organization, Audelco supports its activities through membership fees, contributions, and fundraising affairs. Its activities include giving theatre parties and disseminating information about the Black Theatre and related arts through a bimonthly newsletter. Since its inception, Audelco has regularly organized theatre trips at discounted prices for people in the Black communities. Audiences are taken to see plays presented by smaller community theatre companies as well as the more publicized productions of larger companies. One of BTA's priorities is the presentation of awards for excellence in Black theatre. Audelco has fulfilled this goal by presenting annual awards to those theatre artists whose contributions would probably otherwise go unrecognized. Consequently, Audelco awards have come to mean recognition and have done much to commend efforts by theatre artists who may never receive Broadway acclaim. In addition, Audelco is credited with having developed an audience that is more discriminating, more critical, and more theatrically sophisticated. Vivian Robinson's practical and realistic vision reflects that of the founders of BTA as well as that of past Black Theatre artists: "We realized back then that we are going to have to do for *us*." [6]

BTA continued to grow and by 1977 had eight unbroken years of existence and a membership of fifty-two organizations. Sometime around 1975 it altered its strictly legitimate-theatre policy and began admitting dance companies. Within two years nearly 50 percent of BTA's members were dance companies, including the Alvin Ailey American Dance Theatre. Although BTA spread its umbrella to include more forms of theatre and arts projects, its original purpose has always been to serve member organizations by expanding their base of audience support and raising funds. Because BTA was formed by individual companies with identical interests, needs, and goals, it is seen as an organization that projects the collective image of a Black Theatre and confirms its presence. But an organization, like any living entity, depends for its survival and identity on the singular parts united to make it a whole.

Two significant factors within the Black Theatre Alliance have been the New Heritage Repertory Theatre Company and its founding artistic director, Roger Furman. New Heritage was founded in 1964, but by then Furman had already established himself as a moving force in Black Theatre. Even before the era of the dynamic 1960s this artist, writer, set designer, producer and director had responded to the needs of Black Theatre by organizing the Negro Art Players in 1952. Loften Mitchell recalls in *Black Drama* that Furman's purpose was to bring summer stock to Harlem.[7] This modest venture was ambitiously undertaken with little money and few convinced backers. Mitchell reports that despite obstacles, Furman was successful in negotiating with the Elks Community Theatre to present three one-acters in July of 1952. This bill included Tennessee Williams' *Mooney's Kid Don't Cry*, Furman's own *The Quiet Laughter*, and *The Oklahoma Bearcat* by Charles Griffin. Furman's contributions during this time are even more noteworthy since they were several years in advance of the events and personages credited with launching the Black Theatre Movement. Furthermore, in 1964 Furman served as field supervisor of Haryou, a Harlem-based arts and cultural program which funded LeRoi Jones' epoch-making Harlem Black Arts Repertory Theatre and School. In fact, Mr. Furman's involvement in Black community theatre goes back to the 1940s, when as a very young artist he designed sets for the American Negro Theatre.

Roger Furman orginally formed a group called the New Heritage Players, but later renamed it the New Heritage Repertory Theatre Company. Being somewhat older than most of the theatre artists he worked with during the 1960s, Furman felt no inner pressure to conform to the philosophy of the Black Arts Movement. Thus, denying any inspiration from that sector, he declared his own purpose to be the production of quality plays as a means of communicating with the masses of Black people in the New York area.[8] Consequently, although New Heritage was seriously involved in Street Theatre as a medium serving the liberation struggle, he objected to overly rhetorical, didactic theatre. To preach to people in deprived communities about injustice and inequality is to be redundant, he believes. Street Theatre should emerge out of the communities by using the language and experiences of the people who live there. Furman feels theatre of the street requires a special program of actor training, with emphasis on discipline. Plays should be short, fast, and should deal with such problems as housing, drugs, police-community relations, and welfare.[9] Actors are subordinate to the community, which is both the source of and the actual milieu for the action. A system of on-the-job training permits New Heritage actors to receive training through public performances. The company began in 1964 with a rigorous schedule of daily workshops and rehearsals that culminated in Street Theatre productions.

Three Shades of Harlem, co-authored by Roger Furman and Doris Brunson, was presented by New Heritage in June of 1965. This production was performed at the YWCA on 125th Street and was the company's formal stage debut. Although its staging was more conventional, this work reflected Furman's concept of Street Theatre in that it "was a moving, humorous panorama of the community . . . and told of the community's problems, of its hopes and dreams." [10] Before finally settling down in one place, New Heritage was forced into a peripatetic existence. This journey began in the fall of 1965, when the company accepted an invitation to use space in Public School 124 on 127th Street. Two years later another move took the company to East Harlem and a larger space at Intermediate School 201. In late 1969 New Heritage moved to the location which became its permanent residence—43 East 125th Street. Furman turned what was a veritable wasteland in the form of an empty, dilapidated loft into a well-designed intimate amphitheatre.

Plays presented by New Heritage that were either written or directed by Roger Furman include *Three Shades of Harlem*, with Doris Brunson (1965), *Hip Black and Angry*, original company production directed by Furman (1967), *Renegade Theatre* (1968), *The Gimmick* and *To Kill a Devil* (1970), *Another Shade of Harlem* (1970), and *The Long Black Block* (1972). The Grass Roots Players was the name given to regulars appearing in New Heritage productions. At one time or another, the group contained the following performers: Melody Beal, John Byrd, Charles S. Griffin, Billie Hassell, Annette Jones, Claire Lyber, Murray Middleton, Yvonne Madison, Roger Parris, Lee Phillips, Rose Phillips, Archie Grant.

True to his goal, Furman goes directly to the community to find audiences for his company's productions. Word of new productions is spread primarily through a grass-roots grapevine, since limited funds prohibit commercially bought publicity. Publicity could, however, be gotten through organs dedicated to serving the Black Theatre Movement, such as *Black*

Theatre magazine, published by New Lafayette Theatre. Furman's method of interviewing the audience after each performance is an effective way of acquiring empirical, on-the-spot feedback without relying on analyses from interpretative critics. This way he can assess the success of the production from the point of view of the audience itself. Direct audience contact, moreover, allowed him to personally promote Black Theatre and Black culture and solicit community support.

It would be just as inaccurate to label the Afro-American Studio for Acting and Speech an actor's company as it would be to label New Heritage a director's company, although the Afro-American Studio was founded by Ernie McClintock, an actor who visualized an acting school exclusively for Blacks. This idea was realized in 1966 when the Afro-American Studio was officially incorporated. Emphasis was placed on a system of actor training which stressed observation and the study of Black lifestyles. Actors were prepared through this method to use their own experiences to portray Black characters. But in addition to giving training in theatrical technique, the Afro-American Studio held classes in Black history and culture. Like New Heritage, the company was dedicated to providing quality theatre productions for people in the New York area, principally Harlem.

McClintock began his career as a member of actor Louis Gossett's Academy of Dramatic Arts. After serving briefly as artistic director of the Gossett academy, he formed his own Academy Theatre, where he taught courses in acting and scene study and directed three original plays developed by company members. He also performed around New York in such vehicles as Edward Albee's *Zoo Story* and the Shakespeare Festival productions of *Henry V* and *The Taming of the Shrew*. From these experiences McClintock concluded that a specialized training program for Black actors was needed because the White-oriented training they received inhibited their ability to portray Black characters realistically. He tailored an acting technique based on African and Afro-American body movement and an in-depth study of Black culture. His curriculum included a study of African dance, the speech patterns found in Black music and folklore, Black Theatre history, and Black aesthetics. Such a comprehensive training gives the actor a broad intellectual background as well as a creative perspective from which to work in a distinctively Black theatre. Yet Black actors are not restricted to Black-oriented material, and McClintock is careful to explain that "with careful training and preparation in every phase of theatre technique, the student becomes flexible and versatile in developing this craft and is able to create any role from a wide repertory including Shakespeare, Chekhov, Bullins, and Baraka."[11]

McClintock also realized that the performance of Street Theatre required disciplined actors. The Afro-American Studio, in fact, engaged just as enthusiastically as New Heritage in Street Theatre. In the summer of 1970 McClintock used two trucks and adapted the medieval wagon-stage concept to the streets of New York City. A portable stage was rigged on one truck while the other truck contained a portable generator. The actors used the subway as a means of transportation. Thus, in Brooklyn and other areas of the city, the Afro-American Studio perfomed its original company production of *Where It's At—70*. Combining poetry, pantomime, song, and sketches, this dramatic pastiche presented impressions of city life.[12] Black Pride was emphasized, and lectures were given on drug addiction and other evils that corrupt and alienate those trapped in neglected neighborhoods. Although the performances repeated the same content from community to community, audience reaction varied. Members of the audience were not discouraged from interfering with the actors or the action; in other words, the actual reality of the streets was not prevented from spilling over into the stage reality. Obviously, this blurring of the sharp lines of demarcation between stage environment and the real world could disorient the average actor. McClintock's method for handling this problem was to have the actor view the performance from two distinct perspectives. Specifically, the actor must maintain the artistic standards of the production while responding to the reactions of the audience. It is also vital that the actor of Street Theatre know how to quickly establish a common ground with the people in the audience and know how to identify with them.

In 1968, the company moved to a 100-seat theatre at 15 West 126th Street that it was to remain at for four productive years.

During this period the enrollment at the Studio grew to over two hundred. A professional staff of twelve was hired to teach courses as diversified as karate and voice and diction. By 1971 the number of productions had increased to nine per season. The Afro-American Studio offered a basic actor-training program which consisted of four- to six-week terms of ten weeks each at a cost of $125 per term. In only one year the company outgrew its first permanent home and had to move to more spacious accommodations at 415 West 127th Street. Here the company was within a short distance of Columbia University, the Manhattan School of Music, the Jewish Theological Seminary, and the Union Theological Seminary, as well as Horace Mann High School, Morningside Church, the High School of Music and Art, and the Board of Education Community District Office Number Five.[13] This location had obvious strategic advantages for the company.

To finance its productions and programs, the Studio sponsored and/or took part in community-related concerts, movies, variety shows, and workshop presentations. More substantial funding was obtained through a variety of public and non-public sources. Some of these sources included the Harlem Cultural Council, the John Hay Whitney Foundation, the Louise L. Ottinger Charitable Trust, the New York State Council on the Arts, the National Endowment for the Arts, the Rockefeller Brothers Fund, and the Educational Facilities Laboratories. Contributions were also solicited from private benefactors and donors.

From its inception, the Afro-American Studio was committed to doing Black plays but remained versatile. The company's first production, in 1967, was *Clandestine on the Morning Line* by Josh Greenfield. This production was followed in 1968 by John Herbert's depiction of homosexuality in prison, *Fortune in Men's Eyes*. Productions that same year were Errol John's *Moon on a Rainbow Shawl* and Langston Hughes' *Black Nativity*. Presented during the 1969 season was a small galaxy of plays by Black playwrights that included Douglas Turner Ward's *Day of Absence*, Baraka's *Dutchman*, Gilbert Moses' *Roots*, Bullins' *Clara's Ole Man*, and *Taking Care of Business* by Marvin X. Also part of this repertoire was the company's original production of *Where It's At*.

The production at the Martinique Theatre in 1971 of N. R. Davidson's theatricalized version of the life of Malcolm X, *El Hajj Malik*, brought the company a measure of recognition and acclaim. *New York Times* critic Clive Barnes wrote of the production, "The play is staged with an admirable air of spontaneity by the Afro-American Studio, Mr. McClintock's Harlem school and theatre. And Mr. McClintock's own contribution, meshing the various elements, including the subtly evocative music composed and arranged by William Slater, cannot be too highly praised."[14] The same review, moreover, pointed out the effective "team improvisation" of the acting company. This was testimony to the company's high regard for disciplined acting. Comprising the cast were John Bailey, Woody Carter, Cindy Burroughs, Norman Butler, Lee Cooper, James Harris, Deborah Howard, August Harris, James Lee, Jim Mallette, and Joan Seale.

The cooperation and esprit de corps that existed among the company members were evidenced again in 1971 when the Studio presented the first part of a two-part Amiri Baraka festival. This time graduates of the Studio joined students to form the acting company. Mel Gussow wrote, "The actors submerged themselves in their roles with passionate conviction."[15] Singled out for special attention was Norman Butler, who portrayed the double-dealing pusher in *Junkies Are Full of (Shhh . . .)*. Of the three plays produced, McClintock directed *Junkies*. Helmar Cooper directed *Experimental Death Unit #1*, while Woody Carter was the director of *Great Goodness of Life*. This sharing of directorial responsibility is further evidence of a climate of participatory democracy within the Afro-American Studio.

The reeducation of Black people and the elevation of their consciousness were prime motives that led Barbara Ann Teer to found the National Black Theatre. In a way, Teer was guided in her way of thinking by the same forces that influenced Ernie McClintock. Her experiences as an actress on Broadway and Off-Broadway had disillusioned her toward the theatre establishment, and she doubted it had any serious intention of dealing fairly with the Black theatre artist. In fact, she came to realize that the entire Western theatre tradition was geared toward the exclusion of Blacks. The Western theatre, dominated by slice-of-life naturalism, aimed to please those theatre patrons who wanted to see only plays that reflected their provincial and complacent view of the world. Thus, producers and directors argued that since Blacks played only negligible roles in American society, their presence on stage in other than subordinate parts would belie theatrical realism. Moreover, this same logic was often used to deny Black actors roles in classical and period plays. Blacks were relegated, therefore, to playing only those roles White producers and directors felt they served in real life. So just as conventions and styles become clichéd in a commercial theatre industry, racial stereotypes can as easily become entrenched. Teer wrote,

As a black actress, as long as this condition prevails, I can merely look forward to playing "demanding" roles such as prostitutes, maids, and/or every now and then, just for local color, of course, some form of exotic. . . . If I'm really lucky and can survive the frustrations of this business, when I'm old and gray, I can look forward to playing a strong, forceful, ball-cutting matriarch and the white theatre will continue to profit from my Negritude.[16]

Teer reached the conclusion that if conditions and circumstances for the Black actor were to improve, then Blacks would have to be in positions to make major decisions and to direct their own lives. Only when Blacks could "call the shots" would they be totally self-assertive and self-determined. What was desperately needed, Teer observed, was a salutary atmosphere conducive to experimentation and creativity. These artistic prerogatives allow the artist to feel relaxed and unself-conscious. For Black theatre artists this meant feeling at home in their own community. Teer's advice to them was to go back to the Black community and begin to build a power base. Countering charges that this was a segregationist idea, Teer responded: "Perhaps this is a form of 'separation' (not segregation), but as of now I see no other alternative."[17] This statement was made in a magazine that appeared in April 1968, the same year Teer founded the National Black Theatre (NBT) in Harlem.

Much like the Afro-American Studio, the National Black Theatre is dedicated to improving the cultural and intellectual lives of Black people. Entertainment is not their prime objective. The National Black Theatre, in fact, repudiates conventional theatre forms as well as basic concepts of Western art. More precisely, Teer developed the concept of "God-conscious" art, which is supposedly guided by the creative impulse that emanates from within. Inwardly inspired creativity obliterates artificial boundaries between performer and spectator, between experiences that are lived and those that are imitative. Western art is an accumulation of culturally biased symbols and archetypes that intimidate and inhibit artistic participation by potentially creative Blacks. Although the Athenian dictator Pisistratus encouraged the growth of theatre in 500 B.C. as a means of uniting the upper and lower classes of Athenians, theatre in the West has evolved into a passive, bourgeois pastime. Training people to transcend the limitations of conventional theatre became a goal of the National Black Theatre. By creating a proper environment, NBT proposed to help those people it came into contact with to discover a positive sense of identity and personal acceptance. The experience was intended to allow people to find a sense of wholeness and develop a healthy attitude toward love.

For a theatre geared toward spiritual and psychological transcendence, a unique form of expression was needed to replace conventional art forms. NBT coined the term *ritualistic revivals* to describe what they did. The ritual part is a musical experience of overpowering creative force that entertains and transforms the audience. Combined in these rituals are elements of religion, dance, music, incantation, and the communal experience. The revival side expresses and celebrates the joy of living and provides for both performers and spectators a liberating catharsis. In a return to the quintessence of theatre, NBT has resuscitated the temple in name and practice. Thus the company uses the alternate cognomen Temple of Liberation. The Temple is dedicated to preserving and perpetuating the Black lifestyle in all its richness and is a place where all the cultural and historical archetypes of Black Consciousness merge into a "celebration of life." So that the audience can be confronted with the reality of their lives, NBT re-creates Harlem and its various lifestyles. This practice is reminiscent of environmental theatre, where the spectators are "scene-makers" as well as "scene-watchers." Also, many of Teer's theories are strikingly parallel to Jerzy Grotowski's. Teer has eliminated negative aspects of Western theatre, especially its materialism and ostentation. Instead, she has created a communal, or "family," structure wherein the actor is encouraged to shed his selfish individualism and work in total cooperation with the other members. NBT keeps its salaries low, and its members are compensated by working toward a common "vision." Grotowski, on the other hand, worked from the premise of the "poor theatre" and praised the self-sacrificing "holy actor" over the mercenary "courtesan actor." Actors at the National Black Theatre are called liberators instead of actors.[18]

NBT's peculiar theatrical performance technology requires a highly specialized actor-training. This training program is actually a process, however. The first stage of the process is a form of deprogramming; the term used by NBT is *decrudin*. Realizing that Blacks as a distinct ethnic group in America have been subjected to psychological conditioning to minimize their racial differences, NBT views deprogramming as necessary to restore Black actors and spectators to their proper ethos. The specific intention is to return Blacks to their spiritual base so they can rediscover their individual identities and their collective identity. To accomplish this, each actor must first comprehend, then pass through, five circles of evolution. The levels are more or less successive steps in the development of a "liberator." One can begin at the bottom of the pyramid—"the Nigger," described as materialistic and self-serving—and progress upward. But one can easily start at the highest, most evolved "Revolutionary" level if he or she is already fully capable of dealing with the spirituality of Blackness. In order of importance, the other levels are "the Negro," "the Militant," and "the Nationalist." Ideally, an individual undergoes an internal purgation before external change is undertaken.[19]

During a visit to Nigeria in 1973, Teer found the thread she needed to complete the revolutionary cycle. Her work with Yoruba art in Osogbo, Nigeria, led her to view theatre as an exaltation and celebration of the universal life force.[20] Ms. Teer had made her first trip to Africa on a Ford Foundation grant. But when she returned to Harlem she and the members of NBT, on their own, collected enough money to send the entire company back to Nigeria. While there working with other Nigerian artists, they were inspired to develop a work entitled *Soljourney into Truth*. They took this work to the 1977 Black and African Festival of Arts and Culture (FESTAC) in Lagos, Nigeria. Other productions during NBT's 1977–78 season were *Ritual*, music and lyrics by Barbara Ann Teer and company, *Seven Comes Up Seven Comes Down* by Lonne Elder III and Adeyemi Lythcott, and Alice Childress' *Wine in the Wilderness*. New productions for 1978–79 were *Softly Comes a Whirlwind Whispering in Your Ear* by Barbara Ann Teer and *The Owl and the Pussycat* by Bill Manhoff. *Riding on the Wings of Love*, a musical by Nabii Faison was featured during the 1979–80 season. Moving into 1980–81, NBT presented *Soul Fusion*, a musical collaboration between Teer and Faison, and *The Boiling Marriage* by George McKinley White.

Since its beginning, NBT has been located at 9 East 125th Street, New York City. Barbara Ann Teer continues to be executive producer of the company. For a while, Frederica Teer served as executive director; Zuri McKie later became managing director. Nabii Faison and Lizz Omilami also served as directors in the company. In addition to its theatrical productions, NBT produced a film, *Rise, A Love Poem for a Love People*, and *Rise*, a video. By 1981 NBT boasted an annual attendance of 250,000. Surely of notable significance was Barbara Ann Teer's revisit to Nigeria in 1980 and her renewed commitment to raise the Black Experience to a level of honor and respect.[21]

During its five years of existence, the New Lafayette Theatre (NLT) was one of the most prolific and resourceful of the Black theatre companies. Although similar to most of the other companies, it reflected a particular aesthetic and social philosophy. Pontiff of NLT was director Robert McBeth, who attended Morehouse College in Atlanta and served in the armed forces before studying at the Actor's Studio. There he met another young director, Adam Miller, and they decided to form a regional theatre in which plays about Blacks written primarily by Black playwrights would be presented. This was in the late 1960s, and McBeth was averse to the proposition of integration in the theatre merely for the sake of integration. He believed that too many plays by Black playwrights had been inordinately concerned with Black-White social problems. What was needed, he felt, was "a community of artists and a community of audience that are equal participants in the theatrical event."[22] McBeth also criticized the missionary syndrome prevalent in American society that takes an "outside to inside" approach to social, political, educational, and cultural matters in the Black community. He sensed something distasteful and even destructive in the posture of "advantaged" outsiders bringing educational and cultural enlightenment to the "disadvantaged." There were problems faced by deprived minorities in the inner city, but solutions to these problems, proposed McBeth, would "be developed from within that body of people, using methods and concepts organic to the body."[23]

The New Lafayette Theatre was founded in Harlem in 1966. Consciously reflected in the theatre's name was an attempt to bridge history and re-create conditions of the past. The old Lafayette Theatre had served the Harlem community and in turn was served by it. It was the expressed intention of McBeth to bring Black artists into closer contact with the Black community so they could be reoriented to Black life. He viewed the Black community in a national rather than a local sense. There were Black artists and there were Black communities all over the United States, but there was no point at which they could converge and commune together. The New Lafayette would thus become a mecca to be visited by artists from across the country, who would take back to their communities the inspiration and knowledge gained from their experience. This way, NLT proposed to serve as a "national community theatre." The infrastructure for this cultural nerve-center was composed of forty participating Black artists who were actors, musicians, designers, and technicians. Their singular purpose was to perform at the highest possible level of excellence.

With the acquisition of Ed Bullins, who had been writing and producing plays in San Francisco, as playwright-in-residence, NLT added another philosophical and creative dimension to its structure. McBeth avowed that plays by White playwrights would be accepted as long as they depicted the playwright's experiences with Blacks. Also, plays by socially conscious White writers such as Bertolt Brecht, were acceptable if the experiences they portrayed honestly paralleled those of Blacks, but under no circumstances would plays by Whites about Blacks be welcome. Bullins was in complete agreement with McBeth on the purposes and goals of a Black Theatre and he quickly became a spokesman for NLT. During a forum published in NLT's *Black Theatre* magazine, Bullins explained:

I think as Black artists, we should learn how to come together and form our own institutions, our own vehicles and corporations, to take our talents and give them to the people and to like have something to build upon. . . . This is one thing we are trying to do at The New Lafayette in Harlem. Not only is Black theatre needed, but Black publishing companies, Black film companies, Black radio companies, Black communications that so a Black person never has the excuse that "he had to go some place else and work."[24]

Bullins' vision was realized, but a suspicious calamity befell NLT before it could make its most impressive accomplishments. On January 31, 1968, a fire destroyed the first theatre, which had opened in October 1967 at 132nd Street and 7th Avenue. This particular site had sentimental value since it was the original location of the old Lafayette Theatre of the 1930s. But in December 1968 the company opened a new theatre at 137th Street and 7th Avenue. After this a succession of events occurred. On December 10, 1968, through January 28, 1969, Ed Bullins' *In the Wine Time* was presented. This was followed in February 1969 by a revival of *Who's Got His Own* by Ron Milner. *We Righteous Bombers* by Kingsley B. Bass, Jr., was produced April 18 through June 3, 1969. The first of a series of Black rituals was begun on August 29, 1969, with *A Ritual to Bind Together and Strengthen Black People So That They Can Survive the Long Struggle That Is To Come*. In the middle of all the production activity, in September 1969, NLT launched the New Lafayette Theatre Agency, a non-profit play service that handled the plays of NLT playwrights. After this event, another Bullins play, *Goin' A Buffalo*, was presented October 24 through December 7, 1969. *To Raise the Dead and Foretell the Future*, a Black ritual, began performances on March 6, 1970, and was subsequently published by NLT's publishing division, Black Theatre Publications. Bullins' *The Duplex* ran from May 22 through July 5, 1970, and that August NLT presented "a play without words" titled *A Black Time for Black Folk*. Described as a "New Lafayette creation," *The Devil Catchers* ran from November 27, 1970, through January 10, 1971, and was also published by Black Theatre Publications.[25]

While awaiting the opening of their new theatre, NLT had not been idle. With members of the New Lafayette company, McBeth directed three of Bullins' plays Off-Broadway at the American Place Theatre. The plays which opened in March 1968 were *A Son, Come Home, The Electronic Nigger*, and *Clara's Ole Man*. *Black Theatre: A Periodical of the Black Theatre Movement* had its first issue published in September 1968. Several members of the company's playwriting corps achieved name recognition, especially Richard Wesley, Sonia Sanchez, J. E. Gaines, Ben Caldwell, Marvin X, Sharon Stockard (Martin), and Martha Charles. Whitman Mayo and Roscoe Orman were two of the company's stand-out actors. NLT also offered free acting classes for children aged eight to twelve and provided free theatre tickets to the community and general public. NLT's funding came from the Ford Foundation, the Rockefeller Foundation, the New York Foundation, and from individual patrons.

Although the New Lafayette began with the promise that Black Theatre should draw upon the community it serves for talent and material, critics have alleged that in some ways the organization, rather than living up to its promises to the community, became exclusive and sectarian. Some of the critics even charged that the addition of Ed Bullins as playwright-in-residence made the theatre a virtual showcase for his plays. And critic Larry Neal seemed convinced that the New Lafayette's rituals could not have been done at the Apollo Theatre, where the tastes of the Black masses prevail. In Neal's opinion these rituals wasted creative and artistic energy. He found NLT's rituals to be pretentious and self-consciously pedantic when compared with the National Black Theatre's rituals, which were reported as being grand, highly energized, and functional.[26] NLT was also criticized for wasteful expenditures, for not using the best talent available, and for letting the artistic level of its productions drop considerably. For whatever reasons, NLT in the winter of 1972 voted itself out of existence. For some people this was the end of a glorious epoch of Black Theatre that began in the mid–1960s. Constituting somewhat of a posthumous publication, *The New Lafayette Theatre Presents* was published by Bobbs-Merrill in 1974. The anthology was edited by Ed Bullins and contains plays and aesthetic comments by playwrights J. E. Gaines, Clay Goss, Oyamo, Sonia Sanchez, Richard Wesley, and Ed Bullins.

How to effectively translate theory and idealism into action was a major dilemma faced by Black Theatre artists and writers. This dilemma was manifested vividly in the problems encountered by the Free Southern Theater (FST) during its early years. The nature of the meeting between two of the theatre's original founders had an element of prophetic coincidence. Something similar had occurred between Genet and a Black actor in Paris, an incident that started the playwright thinking about the meaning of Black existence and experience. As revealed in the book *Free Southern Theater by Free Southern Theater*, the first time Gilbert Moses and John O'Neal met they engaged in a debate on tragedy and comedy. O'Neal held that tragic drama was the superior form, while Moses took the side of comedy. There is no mention of a conclusion or agreement being arrived at, but there did continue to be a disharmonious clash of beliefs and ideas among FST's directors and participants.

The formation of the Free Southern Theater was sincere enough. Actually, the idea at the beginning was far from any intentional radicalization of the theatre. To the founders of FST, starting a theatre in the Deep South was a logical step in the movement to produce political, social, and economic changes in the lives of southern Blacks. Their intentions were obviously humanitarian and inspired by a recognition that Blacks in the South were also deprived culturally. This kind of thinking characterized the scores of northern-reared and northern-educated young idealists who went South during the early 1960s to actively participate in the Liberation Movement. Among this group of activists were the organizers of FST. John O'Neal and Doris Derby were field directors for the Student Non-Violent Coordinating Committee (SNCC) in Jackson, Mississippi. Gilbert Moses was a writer for the *Mississippi Free Press* in the same city. They met in the winter of 1963 and subsequently came to the conviction that a theatre in Jackson was not only needed but feasible. As artists, they perceived the rural areas of Mississippi as veritable cultural wastelands. As a remedy, they proposed to create an Athens in Jackson where people could come together for intellectual and social involvement and to celebrate Black culture. A prospectus was drawn up outlining the general plan for a Free Southern Theater. The main objective was the establishment of a "legitimate theatre" in the Deep South located in Jackson, Mississippi, with other objectives as follows:

1. The stimulation of creative and reflective thought among Blacks in Mississippi and other southern states by establishing a legitimate theatre, thus providing the opportunity for involvement in the theatre and the associated art forms.

2. The eventual development from within the Southern situation of a theatrical form and style that is as unique to Black people as the origins of blues and jazz.

3. To produce through a combination of art and social awareness a dramaturgy which will relate to the problems within the Black person himself, and within the Black community.

4. Through theatre, to open up a new area of protest that will enhance the development of playwrights and actors, and also permit the growth and self-knowledge of a Black audience that supplements the present struggle for freedom.[27]

Discernible in these objectives is a commitment to social progress and to an activist strategy. Also, there is voiced a pledge to develop a viable theatre tradition among Black people in the South. Thus, FST was faced with the problem of waging effective protest while simultaneously developing a radical theatre form at a time when the Liberation Movement was guided by a philosophy of non-violence and passive resistance. Furthermore, since the movement was essentially integrationist, another serious problem was finding a way to build a theatre based on Black culture, thought, and reality that could involve White participation. At first, White involvement did not appear to threaten the theatre's objectives. In fact, a White actor named

Murray Levy was the first actor to join FST and, after the ideological upheaval that led the theatre to more fully embrace the concept of ethnic purity, the last White actor to abandon the fold. FST began as a completely integrated theatre that aspired toward artistic and political relevance. From the beginning SNCC used the strategy of integrating its activists into the grass-roots communities and letting them work closely with the people. Likewise, FST proposed to work within the Black community to validate the positive aspects of Black lifestyle and affirm the culture. But since the political verities were urgent, the development of a culturally based aesthetic and repertory of dramatic literature was delayed. In essence, the theatre was caught up in the movement's momentum and was forced to react hastily.

Moving from ideas on paper to an organized, functional theatre was therefore a top priority for FST. The theatre's nucleus was composed of Doris Derby, who served as scenic designer, John O'Neal, a recent graduate of Southern Illinois University, who was in charge of production and organization, and Gilbert Moses, who had some experience in Off-Broadway theatre and was responsible for actor-training. In need of experience and organizational expertise, the founders contacted Richard Schechner at Tulane University. Schechner was then a professor at Tulane and editor of *Tulane Drama Review*. It was through his brother William, a former roommate of Moses at Oberlin College and a reporter for the *Mississippi Free Press*, that Schechner had come to the attention of FST. In the February 1964 letter he received from Moses, O'Neal, and Derby, he was presented with a blueprint for a theatre in the Deep South and was asked for advice on the implementation of the plan. Consequently, Schechner invited O'Neal, Moses, and Denise Nicholas (later to marry Gilbert Moses) down to his residence in New Orleans. Over an April 1964 weekend that involved the four in stimulating and self-revealing intellectual discussions, interracial social interaction, and soul-searching, Schechner decided to join the group and work toward making the theatre a reality.[28] Eventually, over a five-year affiliation with FST, Schechner served variously as producing director, advisor, member of the board, and chairman of the board of directors.

Initially, he was given the responsibility of structuring FST, helping to organize a committee in New York, and assisting in fund-raising. His analysis of FST and his association with the theatre and its people in *Free Southern Theater by Free Southern Theater* presents a strikingly revealing assessment. His analysis is important because of its honesty as well as its illumination of views in opposition to White participation in Black theatre.

An outspoken critic of White influence upon Black theatre ventures is Harold Cruse. His point of view is based on a historical trend of White usurpation of power from Blacks and the dominance of Anglo-Saxon social and cultural prerogatives over those of other American ethnic groups. Basically, his premise is that a Black theatre cannot function as an ethnically pure institution unless its entire operational apparatus is completely controlled by Blacks. Cruse declares: "Negro theatrical history has demonstrated time and time again the inexorability of that unique Negro-white aesthetic, that culturally false symbiosis that undermines and negates the Black theatre idea."[29] Certainly, there was nothing wrong with the FST founders seeking help and advice from White persons who had knowledge of and a facility for theatrical management. Cruse is simply alluding to a social and cultural incongruity between Blacks and Whites that prevents them from successfully submerging their ethnocentrism. Schechner is forthright in admitting: "I was alienated from white culture but could not be part of Black culture."[30] He does confess that during his association with FST he was never allowed to become an integral part of the decision-making inner circle. Still, Schechner played a meaningful role in helping to shape and guide FST during its formative period. Whether he clearly understood what the young activists of FST were trying to accomplish and whether he could identify with them and their problems are not as important as what his involvement reveals about the theatre's lack of clarity. Cruse adds: "If any group of Negroes were to start a black theatre in a black community without a well-thought-out rule of thumb on administration, Negro playwrights, white playwrights, Negro actors, white actors, Negro technicians, white technicians, Negro directors, white directors, Negro audience, white audience, Negro plays, mixed-cast plays, etc.—such a theatre venture would soon collapse."[31]

As it was, FST did not have a criterion for dealing with the dichotomy between a Black-styled theatre and an integrated company and audience. Having to begin somewhere, they fell back on the Theatre of Social Consciousness and the Theatre of Revolt by doing playwrights like Bertolt Brecht, Sean O'Casey, Eugène Ionesco, and Samuel Beckett. Actually, it was in the fall of 1964 that the theatre opened in New Orleans with Martin Duberman's Black History documentary *In White America*. Following this premiere production, during the month of August, the play was presented in fifteen rural Mississippi communities. This initial tour was followed by a second one that lasted from November 1964 through January 1965 and covered over twenty towns in Mississippi and Tennessee. The repertoire included Beckett's *Waiting for Godot* and *In White America*. However, they showed a lack of courage in their selection of a Black play by a Black playwright and selected Ossie Davis' mild *Purlie Victorious* over James Baldwin's fiery *Blues for Mister Charlie*. To motivate the audience to reflection and discussion, FST held open forums at the end of the performances. Since the majority of these rural inhabitants had never before seen a play performed live, these discussions helped them to form a better understanding of and an appreciation for theatre. Also, the occasion gave them the opportunity to articulate their own views on issues that affected their lives. There were even times when these discussions broke through social barriers and brought Whites and Blacks together in an exchange of opinions. Despite this success, FST was still faced with the difficult task of finding suitable plays to produce and the problem of grossly inadequate finances. Neither of these problems, it turned out, was easily overcome.

Not quite a month after the second tour, in February 1965, the entire troupe traveled to New York to raise funds by staging benefit performances. A New York committee had been set up and assisted in the fund-raising efforts. Although scarcely enough money was raised to pay the troupe members, who now consisted of the four original members who remained after the

others defected, and nineteen new recruits, the company outlined plans which included another extended tour, a repertory
company that would travel continually, a permanent community theatre, and workshops for playwrights and actors. For its
third tour, FST's repertoire consisted of *In White America*, Brecht's
The Rifles of Senora Carrar as adapted by George Tabori, O'Casey's *Shadow of a Gunman*, Molière's *George Dandin*, and Baldwin's *Blues for Mister Charlie*. The company's weekly overhead
of $1,000 was offset slightly by the willingness of private indi-
viduals in the towns they toured to supply the troupe with free
room and board. But FST's determination to live up to its name
by offering free admission merely added to its financial woes.
At the same time FST was metamorphosing into an all-Black
theatre, Schechner, with some reservation, became chairman of
the racially mixed, middle-class board of directors. More in the
spirit of altruism than authoritativeness, the New Orleans–based
board of directors aided the company by providing it with food
and lodging, ratifying decisions, making suggestions for fund-
raising, and in desperate times, personally donating lump sums
of $500 or more. As it was, FST's magnanimity worked against
it in that foundations required theatres to be self-supporting as
a condition for funding. Even as early as 1965 the theatre projected an annual operating budget of $98,000 to $100,000. Obviously, some perspicacious thinking was needed to make the
theatre attractive to funding institutions while it was reestab-
lishing itself as a completely ethnic theatre.

FST is important to the Black Theatre Movement because it
was one of the very first theatre companies established during
the era; it is also important because it set an example when it
switched from the ideology of the Civil Rights Movement to that
of Black Nationalism. This move came in the middle of 1965 and
is attributed to the upheaval sparked by the publication of *The
Autobiography of Malcolm X*. The impact of Malcolm X's life and
ideas shifted the sphere of influence in the Liberation Movement from the South to the urban North. As an overt response
to this shift, many activities within the Civil Rights struggle became radicalized and repudiated the doctrine of non-violence
and integration for that of separation and resistance. Consequently, Black intellectuals and rebels looked to the northern

ghettos, instead of the southern towns and plantations, for inspiration and guidance. A second phase of the Liberation Movement, one might say, began at that point. Since the more radical elements of FST found in Black Nationalism the theoretical base that had eluded them, they argued a strong case for reshaping the company around nationalist principles. The strongest challenge for an all-Black theatre was waged by Gilbert Moses, Denise Nicholas, and Roscoe Orman. John O'Neal believed that FST was already an ontological entity and therefore should not fall victim to race doctrine. In other words, instead of being influenced by popular ideas, FST should impress the audiences by displaying its own liberation. On the other hand, the arguments of Gilbert Moses were broader and more complex. He argued first in favor of tapping and putting on stage that element of Black society that ignores, and is ignored by, the American cultural mainstream. Excluded from TV, film, and the theatre, this neglected subculture deserved to have its values, images, and experiences portrayed through some theatrical medium. Moreover, in light of the fact that the American theatre industry remained discriminatory, Black people needed to face the problem by creating theatres in their own communities. In addition, Moses proposed that FST reflect the concept of a theatre for Black people established and run by Blacks rather than follow the White-oriented liberal idea of uplifting the culturally deprived. He further proposed that FST find its direction in Black Consciousness and encouraged the creation of new plays that dealt seriously with the Black Experience. Moses also believed the renaming of FST to Third World Theatre would help the company project a more appropriate image.[32]

Curiously, the metamorphosis of FST from an integrated theatre to a Black theatre was more the result of evolution than revolution. The defection and circumstantial departure of certain key members from the company caused a dissolution within the administrative ranks. It was the height of the Vietnam War, and after receiving his draft notice, John O'Neal filed for conscientious objector status. Following several hearings, he was ordered to do alternative service by working in a children's home in New York. Naturally, this meant that he had to uproot himself from New Orleans. He left in January 1966 to fulfill his military obligation. Gil Moses left FST the spring of that same year. Eventually, Denise Nicholas defected to the Negro Ensemble Company, and Roscoe Orman joined the New Lafayette Theatre. Schechner resigned as board chairman around the same time Moses quit as artistic director. Schechner explains, "I was becoming interested in happenings and environmental theatre and I thought FST was necessary but square."[33] Apart from his personal feelings about FST, Schechner's statement highlights a major difference between the two prominent theatre movements during the era, the Black Theatre Movement and the Radical Theatre Movement. Essentially, the Radical Theatre endeavored to re-create the spontaneous spirit and excitement of primordial drama by rediscovering the past. In contrast, the Black Theatre was basically concerned with recreating a distorted racial image through the realistic depiction of social issues. By alluding to FST as old-fashioned, Schechner underscores the fact that even at the expense of seeming conventional, the Black Theatre Movement most often favored coherence over the abstract.

It can be surmised that the reason FST seemed so much like bourgeois university theatre was because its college-trained and college-influenced architects viewed theatre academically. What the company needed at this juncture was leadership from someone who perceived theatre not with awe and reverence but as a vehicle to further the goal of total liberation. Thus, the addition of Tom Dent to the board of directors was a move in the right direction. On a trip to New York in 1964, Moses and O'Neal met Dent, a New Orleans–born poet and writer who wanted to return home. The FST directors invited Dent to join the company. Subsequently, with the departure of Moses and O'Neal and the resignation of Schechner as board chairman, Dent became chairman of the board. Almost immediately, he began straightening things out administratively and artistically. Finding a solution to the company's race dilemma and clarifying FST's purpose were other major problems Dent faced. Although Dent's first proclamation sounds reiterative of Gil Moses', it is more clearly defined:

Now I feel what we are struggling toward . . . has to do with planting seeds so that the theater can grow in the garden of black cultural consciousness. . . . Blacks already have the richest, most viable, most complex and rewarding culture in this potpourri of America. The battle is not one of bringing culture to black people, but of us learning to value, and affirm, the culture we already have—and, as far as the performing company is concerned, to adapt that culture, that strength, to the stage.[34]

In 1967 FST began an ambitious workshop geared toward playwriting and community-oriented drama. Val Ferdinand became the influential director of the community writing and acting workshop called Blkartsouth. Along with the workshop, the company produced *Nkombo*, a literary magazine. Much like Bullins at the New Lafayette, Ferdinand as poet and playwright emerged as an independent spokesman for FST. Ferdinand advocated less ideas and theories and called for a theatre based on experiences that are tangible and alive.[35] Because FST continued to have administrative problems, Ferdinand, as well as several other company members, assisted Dent with the administration of the company. When O'Neal decided to return to New Orleans in October 1968 and reclaim leadership of the southern board, the conflict wherein O'Neal was director of the New York board, and Dent chairman of the board in New Orleans was resolved. It seems Dent never had a passion for administrative work.

In 1970 the company suffered another major administrative crisis, and due to diminished external financial aid, also suffered a severe financial crisis. Ferdinand, as Kalamu ya Salaam, led Blkartsouth in a breakaway from FST. By 1975, after five years of revising and reaffirming its purposes and goals, FST was determined to depend on the Black community for its survival. Although contributions from the general public that year amounted to around $5,000, that sum did little to defray an annual budget of $100,000. Thus, the company applied for and received a special Rockefeller grant which permitted them to engage Theodore Ward as playwright-in-residence and to produce his historical play *Our Lan'*.

Born out of the Civil Rights Movement, the FST lost much of its financial and spiritual support when the Movement waned during the 1970s. Since O'Neal had been the principal administrator for FST for most of its nineteen years, he was determined to keep it extant. When he began to write and direct for other theatre groups such as The Play Group of Knoxville, Tennessee, he decided that he could not work full-time for FST and that it should expire honorably. O'Neal's popular one-man show, *Don't Start me to Talking or I'll Tell Everything I Know: Sayings from the Life and Writings of Junebug Jebbo Jones*, produced for the first time in 1980 in New Orleans, was the last FST production. After the FST closed, O'Neal said:

FST died in 1982. In 1984, we plan to have an official funeral, which will involve, according to the funds available, a week or two of reviews, in which everyone ever connected with FST will be invited to return and participate in a commentary on the 60's—then we'll have a big party. At the end of the festivities, a box containing a mirror will be borne through the streets of New Orleans with a full jazz band to the Louis Armstrong Park, where the box will be opened, and viewers can pass in procession and view themselves in the mirror inside the box. After that, the box will be taken to the cemetery, where it will be interred, and words said in a final farewell to the Free Southern Theater.[36]

Speaking on behalf of the Negro Ensemble Company, Douglas Turner Ward explains that a significant Black Theatre should "provide a center where Black creative talent could be nurtured and a Black audience built."[37] NEC was founded in the summer of 1967, under the direction of actor Robert Hooks, actor/playwright/director Douglas Turner Ward, and producer/director Gerald Krone. From its beginning, NEC was criticized for its integrated administration, its grant from the Ford Foundation, its theatre in Greenwich Village, and its first season's bill. Clearly, in its nascent stage, the objective of NEC was to survive. The directors selected during the theatre's early days Peter Weiss' *Song of the Lusitanian Bogey, Summer of the Seventeenth Doll* by the Australian playwright Ray Lawler, and Nigerian playwright Wole Soyinka's *Kongi's Harvest*. These plays reflected the Black Experience, but they were not written by Afro-American playwrights. As the company developed, the directors produced more Black-authored plays, but they continued to repudiate revolutionary plays, feeling revolutionary plays were, simply, "bad plays." Douglas Turner Ward emphatically stated his position:

I had had my years of handing out leaflets on street corners, writing for the *Daily Worker*. I didn't want the leaflet-writing kind of thing any more. . . . I had reached the point at which I felt this strong desire to deal with the Black Experience in all its complexity.[38]

Ward must have felt that the style best able to depict the Black Experience in all its complexity was naturalism, for NEC soon started producing naturalistic plays. According to Ward, these were plays Black audiences wanted to see because they could closely identify with the aspirations of the characters. NEC produced a line of successful plays, all more or less naturalistic "evocations of Black family life," most notably Lonne Elder III's *Ceremonies in Dark Old Men* (1969), Philip Hayes Dean's *The Sty of the Blind Pig* (1971), Joseph Walker's *The River Niger* (1972), and Leslie Lee's *The First Breeze of Summer* (1975). However, NEC did not restrict itself to naturalistic family dramas, although this type of play did do well commercially. In an effort to live up to its promise to introduce new playwrights and actors, to develop new resources, and to explore uncharted aesthetic frontiers, the company experimented with plays that varied in style, form, content, and perspective. The range of styles extended from the symbolic realism depicted in John Scott's *Ride a Black Horse* (1970–71) to Lennox Brown's use of symbolic expressionism in *A Ballet behind the Bridge* (1971–72). After mildly rebuking NEC in *The Drama of Nommo* for ambivalently capitulating to White standards, Paul Carter Harrison received a production in 1973–74 of his "cosmic focused" ritual, *The Great McDaddy*.

Events that culminated in the formation of the Negro Ensemble Company began in 1965–66 with the production of two of Douglas Turner Ward's one-act plays, *Happy Ending* and *Day of Absence*. The production of Ward's plays of social satire ran for fifteen months Off-Broadway and was a popular and critical success. Robert Hooks was the producer, Gerald Krone became the production manager, and Philip Meister, who five years earlier had been unsuccessful in raising enough capital to produce the plays, was the director. As a result of the attention his plays engendered, Ward was asked by the *New York Times* to write an article on the Afro-American in the theatre. Titled "American Theatre: For Whites Only?" the article appeared in the *New York Times* on August 14, 1966. Ward was articulate and emphatic in stressing the need for an established Black Theatre, declaring,

For the Negro playwright committed to examining the contours, contexts and depths of his experiences from an unfettered, imaginative Negro angle of vision, the screaming need is for a sufficient audience of *other Negroes*, better informed through commonly shared experience to readily understand, debate, confirm or reject the truth or falsity of his creative explorations.

Ward explained further that while Blacks would be the primary audience, Whites need not be excluded. Just as a bourgeois English drama had been invigorated by the obtrusion of lower-middle and working classes, Black participation was viewed as offering a potent infusion of life into a moribund American theatre. More practically, the theatre Ward envisioned would not just train actors for an uncertain commercial theatre but would be both a training center and a permanent home for displaced Black actors, playwrights, and technicians.

It is believed that Ward's *Times* article attracted the attention of officials at the Ford Foundation, motivating them to recommend a grant for such a theatre. A formal proposal was written up and submitted, which Ford accepted. Along with co-founders Robert Hooks and Gerald Krone, Ward eventually received a Ford grant of $434,000 to establish the Negro Ensemble Company. A nucleus already existed in the form of Hooks' three-year-old Group Theatre Workshop. There was therefore no problem in finding a talent pool. Since the St. Mark's Playhouse at 133 Second Avenue had been the site of Ward's successful playwriting debut, he and his co-founders decided to make the theatre the permanent home of NEC. A clearly defined policy established the company as a Black-oriented, Black-controlled theatre of high professional standards with an extensive training program in all facets of theatre, from acting to backstage crafts. NEC began its career in January 1968 with a production of Peter Weiss' polemic on Portuguese colonialism, *Song of the Lusitanian Bogey*. Generally, critics agreed that the production was skillful and intense, overshadowing the mediocrity of the script. It was this polished and poised production that impressed the critics and the public, established NEC's credibility, and gave reason to believe Blacks *could* control their destiny in the theatre.

Much of NEC's success, however, was clouded by adverse criticism. Some White critics condemned the Ford Foundation for encouraging Black theatre groups to remain segregated. These critics maintained that an all-Black theatre company did as much as segregated White ones to impede the integration movement. Such inferences were viewed as suspect by Black spokesmen and brought vehement responses from them. Ironically, rebuttals sometimes managed to castigate White critics while simultaneously criticizing NEC. A good example is Clayton Riley's *New York Times* article "We Will Not Be a New Form of White Art in Black Face." Essentially, Riley accuses NEC of pandering to the foundations and the expectations of White people. He does not feel NEC seriously and honestly depicts Black life. Ward comes under attack for what is perceived as his dictatorial control over the company and his sanctioning of mediocrity through the production of bland, innocuous plays. Riley scoffs, "NEC's most significant gesture would come in the presentation of one proud work offered on its feet, rather than a hundred plays produced in a kneeling position before its dubious benefactors and critics."[39] So, too, Peter Bailey's short article in *Negro Digest (Black World)* of April 1968 takes a long, hard look at NEC and raises a pertinent question in the title "Is the Negro Ensemble Company *Really* Black Theatre?" Bailey cites several factors that he feels disqualify NEC as pure Black Theatre. Supporting the argument is Harold Cruse's definition of Black Theatre as an institution completely controlled by Blacks financially, technically, and administratively. The fact that the Ford Foundation, seen by many to epitomize the capitalist establishment, financed the operation of NEC, meant the company could not lay claim to financial independence. Furthermore, since NEC had installed Whites in the key positions of director of training for the professional company, legal counsel, and accountant, neither could the company claim to have full technical and administrative control. Perhaps even more of a repudiation of its credibility as Black Theatre was Bailey's charge that NEC lacked a coherent cultural or Black Nationalist ideology. These factors and the fact that NEC had chosen to exist outside the Black community left the company with hard decisions to make about its identity and purpose.

Perhaps in capitulation to strong ethnocentric pressure, NEC's 1968–69 season was highlighted by a series of Black-oriented, Black-authored plays. To commemorate its second season (1969–70), NEC presented *God Is a (Guess What?)* by Ray McIver and Lonne Elder III's *Ceremonies in Dark Old Men*. Featured also was a bill of one-act plays which included *String* by Alice Childress, *Contribution* by Ted Shine, and *Malcochon* by Derek Walcott. *Man Better Man* by Errol Hill and a European tour finished off the season. Clearly, a precedent was set this second season, for the company went on to produce new plays by young and previously unknown Black playwrights. In a decade, NEC had compiled a stellar roster of playwrights that listed the names of Lonne Elder III, Joseph A. Walker, Paul Carter Harrison, Leslie Lee, Philip Hayes Dean, Derek Walcott, Wole Soyinka, Lennox Brown, John Scott, Silas Jones, Judi Ann Mason, Steve Carter, Charles Fuller, Gus Edwards, and Samm-Art Williams. Besides promoting playwrights, NEC has boosted the careers of many actors and actresses, some of whom went on to achieve greater exposure in film and television. At one time or another the following performers were members of the Negro Ensemble Company: Moses Gunn, Francis Foster, Adolph Caesar, Denise Nicholas, Roxie Roker, Esther Rolle, Rosalind Cash, David Downing, Judyann Elder, Arthur French, Hattie Winston, Clarice Taylor, and Ron O'Neal. Others who performed with NEC are Stephanie Mills, Cleavon Little, Richard Roundtree, Lauren Jones, and Roscoe Lee Browne. A large portion of contemporary Afro-American dramatic literature has come from NEC productions. And, most certainly, the artistic quality of many of those productions was enhanced by designers such as Edward Burbridge. Before going on to design for Broadway, the movies, and television, scene designer Burbridge worked with

NEC on such shows as *The Lusitanian Bogey* and the road company production of *The River Niger*. Just as the Free Southern Theater had done several years earlier, NEC in the year 1978 faced the reality of possible extinction and decided to devise constructive plans to ensure its survival. New programs were instituted to revitalize and reinstitutionalize the organizational structure. Through development projects, production activity was increased and strengthened. While a complete overhaul of the administrative and artistic staffs was effected through changes in personnel, the corporate board was expanded. Professionals were hired to administer a special developmental project, attract outside support, and ensure the institution's stability. Although classroom instruction was replaced by an apprenticeship program and on-the-job training, the company expanded its playwrights' unit and continued its commitment to the discovery of new playwrights. Certainly, NEC demonstrated its interest in showcasing the works of young Black playwrights with its "Works in Progress" program for the 1971–72 season. Playwrights from other theatre companies were asked to participate, and by presenting the plays of Ed Bullins, Martie Charles, and Sonia Sanchez, NEC used the occasion to show its impartiality and nonsectarianism. Nor was the company indifferent toward other mediums of entertainment, especially television, which broadcast *The First Breeze of Summer* (WNET) and *Ceremonies in Dark Old Men* (ABC). A film version was made of *The River Niger*, but since NEC was allowed only minuscule input, the company escapes blame for the movie's artistic and commercial failure.

On July 28, 1980, NEC moved to a larger theatre farther uptown at 424 West 55th Street. But the company's first major production in the new Theatre Four facility was not until October 20, 1980, when Samm-Art Williams' *The Sixteenth Round* was presented. Mel Gussow of the *New York Times* gave the play and the performance a less than enthusiastic review. Although opening night had been postponed while the script was shortened and some roles strengthened, it seems the play was still not ready for production. That aside, NEC saw the move as a renaissance of sorts. The main goal was to make the theatre company, at least, completely self-sufficient. Consensus among NEC members was that the company should try to get along on box-office receipts and subscriptions rather than foundation largesse. Nonetheless, the company expected to receive a $300,000 grant from their biggest benefactor, the Ford Foundation. By 1980 Ford had granted NEC nearly $2 million. Still, the company felt it could generate enough income to maintain its self-sufficiency by raising ticket prices, producing mainly established playwrights, and by depending on its new location to attract a larger, mixed audience.

A year before NEC's historic move uptown, Douglas Turner Ward represented the company in Zambia, Central Africa. For two weeks during the summer of 1979 Ward directed a project jointly sponsored by the Zambian government and the International Theatre Institute of Paris. Working in a village not far from the Zambian capital of Lusaka, Ward helped young African actors prepare skits designed to entertain and educate the villagers. In the African tradition of combining art and everyday life, Ward's group attacked the problem of water sanitation. Although the solution—to sanitize water by boiling it—seems simplistic, the opportunity alerted Ward to novel and relevant ways in which traditional theatre can be adapted to non-Western cultures.[40] In agreement with the attitude of Ernie McClintock and Barbara Ann Teer, Ward feels that aspects of African culture can broaden the scope of NEC's work.

Motivation for the Black Theatre Movement came from a collective protest against America's indifference toward the ethnic and cultural pride of African descendants, but the movement's inspiration was nurtured by a myriad of individuals of different backgrounds and ideals. Vinnette Carroll, for example, was an educator and clinical psychologist before organizing the Urban Arts Corps (UAC) in 1967. Also a talented actress, director, and producer, Carroll wanted to find a way to end the alienation of disadvantaged artists by bringing them into the cultural mainstream and by putting them in closer touch with their community. From the beginning, Carroll realized the advantage of using the musical form along with plays and poetry readings to involve minority groups in cultural events. What began as a summer ghetto arts program backed by the New York State

Council on the Arts, the UAC quickly grew into a full-fledged theatre organization that developed its own works and trained Black and Puerto Rican artists for the professional theatre. After settling into a permanent residence at 26 West 20th Street in Manhattan's Chelsea district, UAC went on to develop and perform several outstanding musical creations, the most popular and successful of which was *Don't Bother Me, I Can't Cope.* This medley of music and songs was a collaborative effort between Carroll and Micki Grant, who wrote the music for this show and numerous others developed by UAC. *Cope* was performed for the first time in October 1970 and moved to Broadway in April 1972. Another UAC product that eventually reached Broadway was *Your Arms Too Short to Box with God.* As part of the 1979 Black Theatre Festival—USA, sponsored by Hazel Bryant and New York's Richard Allen Center for Culture and Art, UAC led off with *When Hell Freezes Over I'll Skate,* Carroll's folk, gospel, and contemporary music rendition of Black poetry. By no means, however, is UAC's scope limited either by or to musical theatre. Carroll's expressed goal is to instill within the artists she trains a desire to achieve excellence, high values, and a sense of commitment to their art and the people they represent. To cultivate these qualities, artists are advised to tap their communities for the vast range of experiences and artistic resources available there. While depiction of the Black Experience is the major focus, Carroll believes it is just as important to illuminate broader human issues. Therefore, for the 1977–78 season at UACT, a decision was made to emphasize the classics, dramas, and the adaptations of folk tales as well as musicals.[41]

To stimulate the growth of Black and Third World playwrights and to help them develop their craft, Garland Lee Thompson founded the Frank Silvera Writer's Workshop (FSWW) in 1973. As a playwright, Thompson used the workshop to provide other aspiring writers with a forum where they could hear their plays read and discussed, receive workshop productions, and participate in seminars conducted by established professionals. Located at 317 West 125th Street, FSWW was formed in commemoration of the work done by the late actor Frank Silvera at his Theatre of Being in Los Angeles.[42] With the 1982 production of Thompson's *Tut-ankh-amen, the Boy King*, FSWW revealed an interest in exploring new possibilities by combining history and documentary drama. This interest was further evidenced in *Jesse and the Games: "Jesse Owens Olympiad,"* a 1983 presentation also written by Thompson and performed during the month of June in the Schomburg Center's outdoor amphitheatre.

Most of the prominent Black Theatre companies were located in New York City. This is not surprising, and was probably no accident, given the fact that New York is the theatre capital of America. What is significant is that the majority of these companies were in Black communities, a sizable number of them in Harlem. But there were also theatre organizations outside of New York that made major contributions to the movement and, because they were regional, helped broaden the national dimensions of Black Theatre. Concept-East was formed in 1962 by producer/director Woodie King, Jr., and playwright Ron Milner. Located in Detroit, Concept-East was launched with out-of-pocket funds put up by the company's founders. When King decided in 1964 to migrate to New York, Milner assumed leadership and kept Concept-East alive and vital to Detroit's Black community. Chicago had the Kuumba Workshop under the directorship of actress Val Gray Ward. As an offshoot of the Watts Writer's Workshop, out of which came *Big Time Buck White* in the late 1960s, the Frederick Douglass Creative Arts Center (FDCAC) was founded in October 1971 in New York. Under the direction of playwright and screenwriter Fred Hudson, FDCAC's mission was to culturally enrich the community with professional theatre and to develop Black writers while giving them exposure. Now directed by Mike Malone, Karamu House has continued to stimulate and educate the minority communities of Cleveland. Founded in 1916, Karamu's continued existence attests to the longevity and continued survival of Black Theatre in America.

NOTES

1. Robert J. Wilson, *The Black Theatre Alliance: A History of Its Founding Members*, Ph.D. dissertation, New York University, June 1974 (Mi-

crofilm SC R–1700, Schomburg Collection, Schomburg Center for Research in Black Culture, New York), p. 16. The majority of information on the Black Theatre Alliance and its member companies comes from this work.

2. *Black Theatre Alliance, Newsletter No. 1* (Schomburg Collection, Schomburg Center for Research in Black Culture, New York): 1.

3. *Black Theatre: A Periodical of the Black Theatre Movement*, no. 5 (1971): 32.

4. McCandlish Phillips, "Message of Street Theatre Is Strong," *New York Times*, 22 June 1971, p. 28.

5. Wilson, *The Black Theatre Alliance*, p. 274.

6. Marilyn Milloy, "Vivian Robinson: Giving Black Theater a Boost," *Essence*, September 1982, p. 15.

7. Loften Mitchell, *Black Drama: The Story of the American Negro in the Theatre*, (New York: Hawthorn Books, 1967), p. 154.

8. Phillips, "Message of Street Theatre," p. 28.

9. Wilson, *The Black Theatre Alliance*, pp. 52–56.

10. Mitchell, *Black Drama*, p. 208.

11. Wilson, *The Black Theatre Alliance*, p. 74.

12. McCandlish Phillips, "In Summer, Shows Take to the Streets," *New York Times*, 27 August 1970, p. 42.

13. Wilson, *The Black Theatre Alliance*, p. 72.

14. Clive Barnes, " 'El Hajj Malik' Staged at the Martinique," *New York Times*, 30 November 1971, p. 57.

15. Mel Gussow, " 'Junkies,' Most Adept, Hits at Drug Evils," *New York Times*, 20 September 1972.

16. Barbara Ann Teer, "The Great White Way Is Not Our Way—Not Yet," *Negro Digest (Black World)*, April 1968, p. 25.

17. Ibid., p. 29.

18. Jessica B. Harris, "The National Black Theatre: The Sun People of 125th Street," *The Theater of Black Americans*, Vol. II, ed. Erroll Hill (Englewood Cliffs, N.J., 1980), pp. 85, 88, 89.

19. Ibid.

20. Mel Tapley, "Barbara Ann Teer Revisits Africa," *Amsterdam News*, December 1980.

21. Laura Ross, ed., *Theatre Profiles 5* (New York: Theatre Communications Group, 1982).

22. Robert McBeth, "Statement," from the program of the New Lafayette Inaugural Season, 1967–68 (Microfilm, Schomburg Center Clipping File, Schomburg Center for Research in Black Culture, New York).

23. Robert McBeth, *Black Theatre: An on the Spot Report, The New La-*

fayette Theatre (Microfilm, Schomburg Center Clipping File, Schomburg Center for Research in Black Culture, New York).

24. *Black Theatre: A Periodical of the Black Theatre Movement*, no. 5 (1971): 33.

25. *Historical Precis*, The New Lafayette Theatre (Microfilm, Schomburg Center Clipping File, Schomburg Center for Research in Black Culture, New York).

26. Abiodun Jeyifous, "Black Critics on Black Theatre," *Drama Review* 18 (September 1974): 44.

27. Thomas C. Dent, Gil Moses, and Richard Schechner, eds., *The Free Southern Theatre by the Free Southern Theatre* (Indianapolis: The Bobbs-Merrill Co., 1969), pp. 3–4.

28. Ibid., p. 209.

29. Harold Cruse, *The Crisis of the Negro Intellectual* (New York: William Morrow and Co., 1967), p. 536.

30. Dent, et al., *The Free Southern Theatre*, p. 209.

31. Cruse, *The Crisis of the Negro Intellectual*, p. 567.

32. Information in this section culled from Dent, et al., *The Free Southern Theatre*.

33. Ibid., p. 222.

34. Ibid., pp. 232–33.

35. James V. Hatch and Ted Shine, eds., *Black Theatre USA: 45 Plays by Black Americans, 1847–1974* (New York: The Free Press, 1974), p. 865.

36. Interview conducted via telephone with John O'Neal, New Orleans, Louisiana, 24 September 1983.

37. Elenor Lester, " 'We Exist to Create a Real Black Theatre': Seasons with the Negro Ensemble Company," *New York Times*, 2 March 1975, sec. 2, p. 5.

38. Ibid.

39. Clayton Riley, "We Will Not Be a New Form of White Art in Black Face," *New York Times*, 14 June 1970, sec. 2, p. 2.

40. "Negro Ensemble Company Lives On," *Africa*, July 1980, pp. 73–74.

41. Ross, ed., *Theatre Profiles 5*.

42. Ibid.

4

Hustling the Muse: The Black Producer

When the prototypical Mr. Brown launched the African Company as a bona fide theatrical producing enterprise, he became the company's first playwright with *The Drama of King Shotaway*. Historically, Mr. Brown's play is recognized as the first play by an Afro-American playwright. Since Mr. Brown presumably contributed the play, lined up the personnel to put on the production, provided the facilities in which to stage it, and succeeded in getting the financing, recognition can also be given to him as the first Afro-American producer. Indeed, Dr. Thomas D. Pawley concludes that " 'James' Brown . . . actually wrote and produced the first [Afro-American] drama in 1823."[1]

Blacks learned early that if they wanted to define their role in the American theatre, they would have to establish their own theatres and theatre companies. Curiously, although the introduction of the Afro-American-authored play was made as early as 1823, Black theatre companies did not always feel obligated to produce only Black works by Black playwrights. Nevertheless, it was quite obvious that if Black theatre companies were to exist, they would have to take the initiative and find the means to produce their productions. Moreover, any innovative vehicle by Blacks depended on Black support to get produced. Often, Black theatre artists combined their talents to create an outstanding show only to discover they lacked adequate financial resources to bring the product before the public. Such a case was the monumental 1921 musical review *Shuffle Along*, whose shoestring budget barely got it off the ground.[2] James Weldon Johnson in *Black Manhattan* reports that after a series of near disasters and embarrassments, F. E. Miller, Aubrey Lyles, Eubie Blake, and Noble Sissle eventually reached Broadway with *Shuffle Along* but only after a circuitous round of Black theatres in Washington and Philadelphia. However, it was the 1898–99 Black musical comedy *A Trip to Coontown* that established the style continued by *Shuffle Along*. That trend-setting show was the creation of playwright/performer Bob Cole and, according to Johnson, was the first all-Black show to be written, directed, produced, and managed by Blacks (if one discounts *King Shotaway*).

From 1910 to 1917, during what Johnson describes as the intermediate period, Black producers such as Whitney Tutt and J. Homer Tutt, Irving C. Miller, and S. H. Dudley sought to keep alive in Harlem the fading tradition of minstrel-styled farce and riotous musical comedy. Although Johnson does not state so clearly, he does imply that the show Florenz Ziegfeld bought the rights to in 1913, *Darktown Follies*, was not only written by Leubric Hill but produced by him as well. In 1928 Frank Wilson wrote and Lester A. Walton produced the play *Meek Mose*. But of all the efforts to get a fair hearing for a theatrical work by a Black writer, the anecdote Johnson tells of Garland Anderson's self-motivated campaign to produce *Appearances* is the most remarkable and prophetic. Story has it that Anderson, a San Francisco bellhop and elevator operator, wrote *Appearances* at the behest of friends and customers at the hotel where he worked to dramatize Christian Science doctrines. In order to get the play staged on Broadway, the playwright sent a copy of the manuscript to President Coolidge, journeyed to New York in a futile effort to get backing from Al Jolson, rented a ballroom at the Waldorf-Astoria and gave a reading for six hundred people. After finally selling shares in the show and lining up enough backers in San Francisco, Anderson and an entourage of supporters motored to New York in two automobiles flying streamers that read "San Francisco to New York—For the Opening Production of *Appearances*—By Garland Anderson, the San Francisco Bellhop Playwright."[3] *Appearances* opened on Broadway in 1925, played a short run, and thus became the first full-length play by an Afro-American playwright to be produced on Broadway. Just as importantly, Anderson showed that it takes undaunted determination and an unself-conscious willingness to appeal directly to all classes of people to support Black Theatre.

The practice of Black theatre companies producing their own shows seemed to hold true as long as the productions were small or were presented to Black communities. Often these turned out to be merely showcase productions, for after they had been tested on Black audiences and proven marketable, White producers were willing to risk taking them downtown. A good example is that of the American Negro Theatre (ANT) under the direction of Abram Hill, Austin Briggs-Hall, Frederick O'Neal, and Hattie King-Reeves. In the 1940s ANT produced a number of exceptional plays in its modest basement theatre at 135th Street before succumbing to success when its revised version of *Anna Lucasta* was taken to Broadway in August 1944. In 1952 playwright Julien Mayfield teamed up with Maxwell Glanville and formed a production company that helped Ossie Davis win recognition with *The Big Deal* (1953), a play expanded from the earlier one-act play *Alice in Wonder*, and retitled.

In *Black Drama* Loften Mitchell relates a personal experience that further reveals problems encountered by Black producers.[4] Mitchell had been asked by musician/composer/songwriter Page Burgie to collaborate with him on a musical, one that would highlight Burgie's talent for writing folk music and his interest in West Indian culture. The result of this collaboration was the musical *Ballard for Bimshire*, which tells the story of a sensitive teenage girl growing up in her beloved Barbados. Because he wanted Blacks to have complete control of the show, Burgie formed a production company called Page Productions that included Ossie Davis, Sylvester Leaks, Ewart Guinier, and Loften Mitchell. Conceding the need for a second party to reinforce efforts to raise funding, Burgie enlisted his accountant as co-producer. However, after the co-producer, Bernard Waltzer, had raised the remaining capital to produce the show, a conflict between him and Burgie developed over artistic control. The dispute was settled when Waltzer agreed to accept an indemnity against budget overruns. Still, in spite of internal dissension among members of the cast and crew, *Ballard for Bimshire* opened in 1963, but it was forced into an early closing because of insuperable expenses.

Social and economic conditions facing Black theatre artists still had not changed very much when the Black Theatre Movement of the 1960s emerged. In fact, during the thirty-five years between 1929 and 1964, ten black playwrights were produced on Broadway. Among that small group, only Langston Hughes and Lorraine Hansberry reached Broadway with more than one play. Still, the 1960s saw the emergence of a number of fine Black actors and directors, exciting playwrights and theatre companies, and energetic producers. However, new approaches were needed to meet the challenges of producing outspoken theatre in a period of social revolution and corporate co-optation. Moreover, non-commercial theatre organizations had to declare themselves non-profit-making and prove their social and cultural responsibility to the community before funding was made available through private and public agencies. Thus, proposal writing and business management were competencies new theatre managers and producers had to master. Many directors of Black Theatre were encountering the world of business and administration for the first time and had to develop their acumen by trial and error. Some, more naturally predisposed toward art than business, made unfortunate mistakes. One such case is LeRoi Jones' Harlem Black Arts Repertory Theatre and School, which in 1965 had its Rockefeller Foundation grant revoked because of alleged discrepancies between the organization's status as non-profit, community theatre and its militant, antiestablishment rhetoric. On the other hand, Black Theatre directors were often derided by the more dissident factions in the Black community for stooping to accept funds from the establishment.

The appearance of the professional Black theatre producer during the 1960s and 1970s was a response to Black Theatre's need for individuals not only competent in business and management but also committed to presenting a truer picture of the Black Experience from a totally Black perspective. Certainly, not all of these producers came from the same background or espoused identical philosophies and beliefs about the theatre as an industry and business. Although practically all of them began their careers by producing Black plays, some moved on to produce works by other ethnic groups, while others kept a commitment to Black Theatre. A few of the professional Black producers were content to devote full time and energy to producing plays, but there were those who combined writing and directing with producing.

Producer/writer/director Woodie King, Jr., actually began his career in the theatre as an actor. According to biographical accounts, King was born in Mobile, Alabama, but at age five migrated with his family to Detroit, Michigan. After completing high school in 1957, he entered the Will-O-Way School of Theater in Bloomfield Hills, Michigan. King's acting career, however, began in a 1957–58 Grosse Pointe, Michigan, production of *Green Grow the Lilacs*, in which he was the only Black performer. And although no other Black students were enrolled at Will-O-Way before he matriculated there, King credits his obsession for the theater to his experience at the school.[5] Rarely used as an actor in school productions, he discovered in the public library the knowledge of theater he was being denied. Later, in 1962, inspired by the mood of the Liberation Movement, King and several Black student actors at Wayne State University, disgusted by the school's discriminatory theatre practices, formed Concept-East Theatre. At Concept-East, King began acquiring the expertise he would use as a successful producer in New York. Also, it was at Concept-East that King and playwright Ron Milner began an association that led to at least two major productions, *Who's Got His Own* and *What the Wine-sellers Buy*. And in 1964 Concept-East moved to New York.

Showing they were not partial to Black writers, Concept-East produced the works of Edward Albee and Jack Gelber as well as those of Baraka, Bullins, and Milner. In 1964 the company took on tour the plays of the Reverend Malcolm Boyd, a White Episcopalian minister who was a committed political activist. Boyd's controversiality helped create interest in the plays, and in New York they appeared at the Union Theological Seminary and the American Place Theatre. These productions made it possible for King to stage five other plays at the nascent American Place Theatre, including the 1965 premiere of Ron Milner's *Whose Got His Own*. His apprenticeship as a producer was enhanced by a John Hay Whitney fellowship, which allowed him to study directing under Lloyd Richards and theatre administration with Wynn Handman, the executive director of the American Place Theater. In addition, King co-founded Theater Genesis at the Off-Broadway Church of St. Mark's-in-the-Bowery. These and other propitious events soon propelled King to a position of influence in the theatre.[6]

In 1965, through actor/producer Robert Hooks, King met the Reverend Adam Clayton Powell and was encouraged by the congressman to write a proposal for a cultural program to be sponsored under the auspices of the federal antipoverty program. Powell helped get the proposal accepted, and $225,000 was allocated to King to establish a cultural training program at Mobilization for Youth on New York's Lower East Side. From 1965 to 1970 the program thrived with vitality and trained young performers in dance and theater, sponsored European tours, and produced early works by playwrights like J. E. Franklin, Lonne Elder III, and Douglas Turner Ward. Filmmaking and television production were also offered through the program. Due to his success, King was invited by the Henry Street Settlement House to head a theater project to be named the New Federal Theater in honor of the WPA-sponsored Federal Theatre of the 1930s.

King formed the New Federal Theatre (NFT) in the summer of 1970, and the theatre's first season was supported by a modest grant from the New York State Council on the Arts and funds provided by the Henry Street Settlement. This debut was made in the basement of Saint Augustine's Church on Henry Street in Manhattan's Lower East Side, where King planned to establish a base and build an audience. Within a few years NFT provided minority theatre for its East Side community and expanded into the greater metropolitan New York area. Shunning racial and cultural parochialism, King produced works by other ethnic groups, such as Jews and Puerto Ricans, thus continuing a policy started at Concept-East. From a meagre first-year budget of $7,500, NFT increased its investment to $300,000 by 1978. Through the Arts for Living Center at Henry Street Settlement, NFT had access to three theatres, rehearsal studios, and up-to-date equipment.

Like those of the New Federal Theatre, King's personal objectives were not based strictly on commercial and financial success but reflected a Black Nationalist approach to America's social problems. King felt a need to support and encourage minority playwrights by giving them an opportunity to see their works produced. Therefore, NFT strove to develop promising theatre talent while providing high-quality theatre productions of interest to its culturally varied audience. Moreover, the company trained members of minority groups for careers in the legitimate theatre and its related fields. To accomplish its objectives, each year NFT staged six to ten showcase productions and held at least four play readings so playwrights could hone their scripts prior to production. Due to a Rockefeller Foundation grant, NFT was able for several years to support a playwright-in-residence. As late as 1976–77, the company offered workshops three times a week in Black and Puerto Rican theatre, and other programs designed to train people in experimental theatre, theatre management, and technical theatre. Further evidence of NFT's community spirit was its Hispanic Playwright Workshop, which presented public play-readings each month.

Between 1970 and 1981 NFT produced more than eleven plays and brought public awareness to such playwrights as Ntozake Shange, Joseph Lizardi, and Ed Pomerantz. An experimental arrangement with Joseph Papp permitted plays to be showcased at Henry Street Settlement then reproduced at one of the New York Shakespeare Festival theatres. Benefiting considerably from this arrangement was Shange's *For Colored Girls Who Have Considered Suicide/When the Rainbow is Enuf*, which went on to Broadway success. However, the first play produced under the agreement was Ed Bullins' *The Taking of Miss Janie* during 1974–75. Chinese-American playwright David Henry Hwang had his *The Dance and the Railroad* staged by NFT at Henry Street then moved to the Public Theatre. Although NFT showcased new plays by unknown writers, it enhanced its professional status by producing old standards, popular revivals, and plays by well-known playwrights. In 1978–79 the company presented *Anna Lucasta* by Philip Yordan, Louis Peterson's *Take a Giant Step*, and Lorraine Hansberry's *A Raisin in the Sun*. The 1976–77 season was distinguished by productions of Owen Dodson's *Divine Comedy* from 1938 and Shakespeare's *Macbeth*, as adapted by Orson Welles and first produced in 1936 by the Negro Unit of the Federal Theatre. The play that brought prominence to the Living Theatre in the early 1960s, Jack Gelber's *The Connection*, was an NFT revival for the 1980–81 season. Besides Dodson and Hansberry, other renowned writers produced at Henry Street were William Branch (*In Splendid Error*), Alice Childress (*Trouble in Mind*), and Ruby Dee (*Take It from the Top*).[7]

King was able to produce *A Black Quartet* after traveling across the country and persuading both Black and non-Black sponsors to invest $500 or more to promote his venture. Of the one hundred people contacted, he organized thirty investors, some of whom put up as much as $1,000. King discovered that ordinary Black people would support Black Theatre if the concept was presented to them in a clear and convincing way. He also concluded that wealthy Black people, like wealthy White people, did not typically back Black Theatre.[8] The success of *A Black Quartet* was a commercial boost for Black Theatre as well as an expression of its more radical ideology. Comprising the quartet were Baraka's *Great Goodness of Life*, Milner's *The Warning—A Theme for Linda*, Ben Caldwell's *Prayer Meeting, or The First Militant Preacher*, and Bullins' *The Gentleman Caller*.

Indeed, King came to epitomize the new mood inspiring the Black Theatre Movement. Writer and critic Peter Bailey credited King with spearheading the Black literary renaissance of the 1960s. Referring to King as the "Renaissance Man of Black Theatre," Bailey wrote, "From community theater in Detroit to a place of influence in national theater and in films, Woodie King has pursued a Black Consciousness theme."[9] Obviously, this belief in racial solidarity and cultural pride has been the force behind King's revolt within the capitalist-controlled American theatre industry. But while providing a source of pride and self-esteem for both Black artists and audiences, cultural militancy has not proven that it can be viable economically. A play with a social message or particular ethnic appeal costs as much to produce on Broadway as a commercial play. As a solution to the dilemma faced by many Black theatres, King suggests that Black artists develop new values and expectations regarding success in the theatre. Simply, Black artists who insist on performing in Black plays for a predominantly Black audience should not expect to receive financial rewards equal to those of artists perfoming before larger, more affluent White audiences. King is critical of those Black playwrights who get production opportunities through Black theatre companies then expect Broadway acclaim. As it stands, producers of non-profit theatre have to continually reinvest profits made on individual shows back into the company. Thus, the company or sponsoring agency can make money, but the producer is not personally compensated. Although Henry Street Settlement received a percentage of the profits from the Broadway and national tour of *For Colored Girls*, King shared only production billing with Joseph Papp. The revenues generated by *Colored Girls*, however, enabled King to produce other shows at the New Federal, and the publicity he received as co-producer of the play boosted his renown and leverage.

Many Black producers believe that Black Theatre cannot survive in New York, where the big-business arena of Broadway is too competitive. Feeling that opportunities for a sustained Black Theatre movement lie outside New York, King established the National Black Touring Circuit. The inspiration for this venture was probably due to the success of Ron Milner's *What the Wine-Sellers Buy*, a show that set a precedent while on national tour. Set in Detroit, *Wine-Sellers* dramatized the attempts of the vainglorious pimp Rico to win the loyalty of a teenager named Steve Carlton who is searching for an identity and a *raison d'être*. Because the action pits Rico against Steve's respectable mother and her admirable boyfriend, many critics dismissed the play as trite soap opera. Milner described his work as an indictment of the capitalist system, which Rico incarnates.[10] Still, this documentary that vividly portrays Black urban life and highlights pimps and prostitutes grossed more on the road than the spin-off Broadway hits *Don't Bother Me, I Can't Cope* and *The Wiz*. Directed by Woodie King, Jr., and starring Dick Anthony Williams, Bill Cobbs, Herb Rice, and Loretta Greene, *Wine-Sellers* opened at the New Federal Theatre in May 1973. Black audiences were favorable toward the play, and it played to packed houses until June. Encouraged by the audience response, King decided to independently produce the play. In October 1973, with the help of Black director Michael Schultz, King staged the play at the Mark Taper Forum in Los Angeles with Glynn Turman in the title role and Schultz as director. In addition, King obtained substantial backing from Joseph Papp to produce *Wine-Sellers* Off-Broadway. With a $200,000 budget, the play opened in January 1974 at the Vivian Beaumont Theatre and ran through March 17, 1974. A summer tour of New York City parks lasted from July to August 1974. Through arrangements with another producer, Moe Septee, King toured the show nationally for a year between November 1974 and November 1975.[11]

Profits from the national tour of *Wine-Sellers* supported King's belief that Black Theatre was marketable in areas outside New York. Actually, the play did well financially in New York before continuing to make money in Washington, D.C., Philadelphia, Detroit, Chicago, and Cincinnati. During its Chicago run at the Shubert Theatre, over 100,000 Chicagoans attended the play and contributed to weekly grosses of between $80,000 and $100,000. The Chicago audiences as well as those in other cities where the show broke house records was 95 percent Black. Popular and financial success of the production was the result of King's shrewd and creative advertising campaigns. Appealing directly and unabashedly to Blacks, the producer advertised in Black newspapers and over Black radio shows. Posters placed in Black communities displayed a flashily dressed Rico, exploiting the penchant of deprived, working-class Blacks for flamboyant and fashionable apparel. At King's request, theatre marquees carried underneath the play's title the blurb "A Black Play for Black People."[12] Against those who objected that the subtitle might be offensive to Blacks and discouraging to White theatre-goers, King used the weekly grosses to defend his strategy. Part of that strategy was to cut costs by advertising in the cheaper Black publications and avoiding the higher-priced White papers, which could carry favorable reviews and still not influence many Whites.

Several Black producers, while opposed to Broadway exploitation of Black musicals, admitted that they could produce a Black musical on a commercial level if it were right for them. Pessimistic about the chances of commercially produced Black Theatre succeeding in New York, King nonetheless staged the 1975 musical adaptation of John Killens' *Cotillion*. Knowing that the

Broadway production cost would equal that of a David Merrick show, King produced the musical at the New Federal Theatre for $15,000 and added another $2,500 per week to keep it going. More importantly, since no admission was charged, these expenditures were somewhat sacrificial. Financing was done through grants, thus permitting those residents of the community who could not afford the luxury of a theatre ticket to see the play. Killens' novel satirizes a range of subjects including the pretentious aspirations of the Black bourgeoisie, the effects of Black Power, and the vapidity of White society. Using characters symbolically named Ben Ali Lumumba and Yoruba Evelyn Lovejoy, *Cotillion* is a parabolic Black comedy. In the title is reflected the novel's underlying theme, the efforts of a Black mother in Brooklyn to get her daughter properly introduced into society. Initially, *Cotillion* had the backing of Motown Records, with Smokey Robinson doing the music, Gilbert Moses directing, and Richard Wesley and Killens writing the script. Each night the New Federal Theatre had to accommodate crowds that exceeded the 300-seat capacity of their theatre. The musical opened in July 1975, played to capacity crowds for three weeks, and closed on August 10. Like other successful productions at New Federal, King hoped an outside producer would pick up the show.

An artist as well as an entrepreneur, King has not been content to devote all his time and energy to producing plays. Besides his success as an actor, he has done well as an editor and anthologist, producer of music albums, and as a film producer and director. Drama anthologies he edited include *The Anthology of Black Drama* with Ron Milner as co-editor. *The Forerunners* was a collection of works by older Black poets like Langston Hughes, Sterling Brown, and Gwendolyn Brooks. *Black Spirits* was also a poetry collection, while *Black Short Stories* anthologized short prose works. A book on the theories, practices, and aesthetics of the Pan-African Movement titled *Black Poets and Prophets* was edited jointly by King and Hal Anthony.

King's first full-length film was *The Long Night*, which he produced in 1975. Based on the novel of the same title by Julian Mayfield, King wrote the screenplay and directed the movie. Exploring the problems faced by Black families in America, the motion picture reveals the experiences of a young boy who stays out all night trying to recover his mother's $27 which was stolen from him.[13] Starring in the film were Dick Anthony Williams, Roger Furman, Sonny Jim Gaines, Woody Jeffery King (no relation to Woodie King, Jr.), Peggy Kirk Patrick, and Shaunelle Perry. Firmly believing that a producer cannot work alone, King formed a joint venture by adding Ed Pitts as associate producer and St. Clair Bourne as co-producer. Funds to produce the film came from Black investors who were persuaded by King's appeal and his explanation of the movie's objective. Subsequently, King produced three films in four years, including the documentary *Black Theatre Movement* which was aired over PBS stations. On the Motown Record label, he produced poetry albums by the Last Poets and Amiri Baraka.[14] In 1971 King produced a three-day poetry festival that featured such poets as Mari Evans, Quincy Troupe, Johari Amini, Clarence Major, Aski Mohammed Toure, David Henderson, Jackie Earley, the Last Poets, Amiri Baraka, and South African poet Willie Kgositsile. Moreover, in 1975 King produced Leslie Lee's *The First Breeze of Summer* for the Negro Ensemble Company and became the first outside producer used by that organization.

More than just an artist and producer, Woodie King, Jr., has definite beliefs and philosophies about Black people in America in general and the Black Theatre in particular. As a spokesman for Black Liberation, he sees Black Theatre as an ideological weapon in the larger struggle for Black progress in a biased society, rather than just a business. As an ideologue, he shares with the members of the Black Arts group the belief that all forms of art should be directed toward Black people with the intention of developing a Black audience. But for Black Theatre to succeed, King believes, it must locate artists who are truly committed and then work outside the context of White unions and White values[15] At the same time, Black Theatre artists must reject European traditions and develop new forms and styles based on the American reality and the Afro-American lifestyle. King believes also that the place for Black Theatre is in Black communities, where Black artists can receive support and be appreciated for their work. But for a Black community art to be relevant, it must be culturally and socially meaningful and reflect Black values.

Whereas Woodie King, Jr., became a film producer and director after achieving success as a theatre producer, Melvin Van Peebles took the opposite route. His *Sweet Sweetback's Baadasssss Song* was more than just a lucky low-budget movie that beat the odds and succeeded commercially and financially. Historically, *Sweetback* and *Shaft*, both released in 1971, are American movie landmarks. *Shaft* also had a Black director, Gordon Parks, and, with *Sweetback*, revolutionized American film content and the tastes of movie audiences. Because these films depicted aggressive Black heroes and heroines triumphing intellectually and physically over symbolic representations of White oppression, they fulfilled the psychological needs of a huge cross-section of Blacks and created a profitable market for the Hollywood "blaxploitation" formula. Certainly, the Black Theatre must have benefited from the enthusiasm of this emotionally charged audience. *Sweetback* realized an estimated $10 million profit on an initial investment of around $500,000, of which $100,000 was Van Peebles' own money. Determined to beat the system, Van Peebles not only wrote the film but served as producer, director, editor, music composer, and leading actor. After *Sweetback*'s success, Van Peebles transferred his talent and business acumen to the stage.

Before making his Broadway debut in 1971 with the production of *Ain't Supposed to Die a Natural Death*, Van Peebles survived an apprenticeship that took him on a circuitous, precarious journey spanning two continents. Born in 1932 on Chicago's South Side, he was the son of a tailor and admits to being raised in a somewhat bourgeois home environment. He grew up in Phoenix, Illinois, a Chicago suburb, and graduated from high school there in 1949. He attended West Virginia State College before transferring to Ohio Wesleyan, where in 1953 he received a B.A. in English literature. Joining the air force after college, he served three and one-half years as a navigator, and after being denied the opportunity by commercial airlines to continue that pursuit, he took up painting in Mexico. A short time later he moved his wife and two children to San Francisco and tried earning a living by working on cable cars.[16]

Van Peebles was working as a cable car gripman when he wrote and published a book that romanticized cable cars. Titled *The Big Heart*, the book was published in 1957 and contained photographs by Ruth Bernhard. Van Peebles believes he was subsequently fired by the cable car management because they resented him for publishing the book. He experienced more resentment and hostility from American publishers who rejected his first novel because it was not typically "Negro," and from Hollywood executives who disparaged his effort to market several short films he had made by suggesting he try tap dancing his way into movies. Disillusioned with America, he expatriated to Europe, where he studied acting in Holland with the Dutch National Theatre and toured the country in Brendan Behan's *The Hostage*. In Paris he discovered that French writers could direct their own movies, so he became a writer and eventually produced five novels, *A Bear For the F.B.I.*, *The Chinaman of the 14th District*, *The True American*, *The Party in Harlem*, and *La Permission* (The Pass). All five novels were originally published in France, but he adapted *La Permission* to the screen and applied for a director's permit, which was granted by the French Film Center. Filmed in French and English, *La Permission* tells of a lonely Black soldier in France, his meeting and brief love affair with a French shop-girl, and their disappointment when a bigoted White American army captain prevents them from seeing each other again. Released in France in 1967, *La Permission* was entered in the San Francisco Film Festival and by 1968 was being distributed in the United States under the title *The Story of a Three Day Pass*. Van Peebles' impressive moviemaking accomplishments earned him a contract with Columbia Pictures. While pursuing his elusive goal, however, he sacrificed his marriage and with it the support and closeness of a family.

Columbia assigned Van Peebles to direct *The Watermelon Man*, a comedy starring Godfrey Cambridge as a bigoted White insurance salesman who awakes to find himself metamorphosed into a Black man. With sarcasm, the movie satirizes racial paranoia and xenophobia, unscrupulous capitalism, and the superficialities of White liberalism. Implicit in the film is the idea "that the urban ghetto for all of its drawbacks is a better place to live than white suburbia." [17] Van Peebles resented having to compromise his artistic integrity to please the Columbia executives and vowed to find freedom as a director.

Sweetback afforded him complete creative control. He acquired capital and backers by going directly to Black investors, and he was able to persuade comedian/actor Bill Cosby to invest $50,000 in *Sweetback* at a time when the production was severely threatened financially. Not only did he learn how to overcome restrictions placed on him by the system, he also learned how to manipulate the system. Like Black writers during the period who used the guise of pornography to delude publishers to the fact that they were making social statements, Van Peebles promoted *Sweetback* as a pornographic film and was able to use non-union workers and amateur actors. Unfortunately, as was the case with *The Life and Loves of Mr. Jiveass Nigger* and *All Night Visitors*, novels by Cecil Brown and Clarence Major respectively, many Black critics and patrons saw only the negative aspects of this movie and failed to discern or appreciate any more meaningful qualities.

Mixed criticism and conflicting opinion also clouded the effectiveness of *Ain't Supposed to Die a Natural Death*. Originally adapted by Paul Carter Harrison from the *Brer Soul* and *Ain't Supposed to Die a Natural Death* recordings of Melvin Van Peebles, the musical revue was directed by Harrison at Sacramento State College in November 1970.[18] At the suggestion of Charles Blackwell, Van Peebles' production associate, a Broadway version of the show was launched.[19] With a production team composed of Gilbert Moses as director, Harold Wheeler as musical supervisor, and Gene Wolsk and Emanuel Azenberg as co-producers, *Ain't Supposed to Die a Natural Death* opened at the Ethel Barrymore Theatre on October 20, 1971. It cost $150,000 to open the show, but since advance sales were dismal, Van Peebles pledged up to $100,000 to cover losses and vowed to contribute more money to keep the show going until business improved. An audience was needed to support the show and guarantee its survival, especially in the face of hostile criticism which caused the usual Broadway audience to stay away. Remembering the overwhelming support he had gotten from Blacks for his *Sweetback* film, Van Peebles took charge of promotion and went about creating a Black grass-roots constituency. To advertise the show, he organized a sales force that sent out publicity to Black churches, schools, social clubs, and fraternal organizations. He even stood outside the theatre and handed out leaflets. Ticket prices were kept reasonable and the advertising campaign in Black communities brought orders for blocks of tickets. The Theater Development Fund committed to buy $10,000 worth of tickets to the show, but later, due to audience interest, increased that amount to $40,000. These tickets were distributed by the fund at half price to schools, colleges, churches, youth groups, settlement houses, and other types of agencies.

The show began to break even around January, but unfortunately, the Shubert Organization requested it be moved from the Ethel Barrymore to make room for other shows. After relocating to the Ambassador Theatre, Van Peebles again elicited help from friends and associates and invited Bill Cosby, Ossie Davis, and Shirley Chisholm to participate in what he called "Black Solidarity behind *Ain't Supposed to Die a Natural Death*." Each performance during the month of January was an event in the celebration of "Black Solidarity," and Van Peebles seized the opportunity to make it appear more than an occasion for entertainment. A write-up in the *New York Times* for December 31, 1971 reads:

Representative Shirley Chisholm, Democrat of New York, will attend the 3 p.m. matinee on Sunday of Melvin Van Peebles' "Ain't Supposed to Die a Natural Death" at the Ambassador Theatre. At the conclusion of the performance, Mrs. Chisholm, who has announced her candidacy for President, will address the audience and discuss "The Black Experience in the Arts and in Politics Today." She will also spearhead a Black community effort to generate support for the Van Peebles production.[20]

The recordings of *Brer Soul* and *Ain't Supposed to Die a Natural Death* are a mélange of poems, speeches, and lyrical monologues. These various forms of vocal expression are bridged together with music that has rhythm and beat but is often rough-edged and unmelodious. Van Peebles' recitations fully utilize the elements of pitch, rhythm, and stress to create an authentic Black vernacular. Devoid of a single plot or story, the recordings reveal characters who soliloquize about their experiences and predicaments in a world that exploits, debases, and dehumanizes them. To develop his primary theme that Black people are the victims of a corrupt and racist system, Van Peebles finds his subject matter and subjects among the pimps, prostitutes, homosexuals, alcoholics, beggars, thieves, and sadistic policemen who invariably inhabit urban communities. To bring these characters to life on stage, Van Peebles and Gil Moses had to elevate them above blatant stereotypes and make them individualistic and dynamic. Since critics were so sharply divided, the show seems to have fallen short of achieving this dimension. Perhaps the severest repudiation came from Eugenia Collier, who wrote in *Black World*:

I left the theatre highly disturbed. The show is a shallow treatment of profound trouble. Van Peebles has disguised in modern garb the same old false image of Black people which white America finds comfortable. And it is evident that the show is written to please a white audience. . . . At best, Van Peebles is a luxury we can't afford. At worst, he is a menace to our selfhood. In any case, he is working against liberation.[21]

Writing in *Essence* magazine, Maurice Peterson lauded the show for its revolutionary form and stated, "It is not hard to figure out why the New York white press has come down so heavily on this beautiful show. . . . It does not work within the conventional devices of Western drama; white people therefore don't have a frame of reference."[22] In the same issue of *Black World* that carried Collier's review, Peter Bailey praised the show for being uncompromising in its depiction of an unsavory side of Black American life, and also expressed appreciation for what he saw as a protest against the people and practices that create these conditions and perpetuate them.[23] On the other hand, Clive Barnes compared the musical to "an opera with recitative and no arias," but found that it had "a strong dynamic force." Somewhat strangely, he described feeling as if he had been transported to another country, and concluded, "Many Broadway theatregoers will not understand what it is saying nor appreciate the almost operatic free style of the way it is being said."[24] Generally, the show received praise for its stunning set by Kurt Lundell, its dazzling costumes, captivating music, and superb acting by a cast that included Dick Williams, Gloria Edwards, Joe Fields, Barbara Alston, Ralph Wilcox, and Minnie Gentry. Nonetheless, *Ain't Supposed to Die a Natural Death* closed on July 30, 1972, after running for 325 performances but without repaying the backers' investment. Van Peebles lost $85,000 of his own money on the show.

At one point, Van Peebles demonstrated his fecundity as an artist and producer by running two Broadway shows simultaneously and completing the film version of one before it opened on stage. *Don't Play Us Cheap* premiered at the Ethel Barrymore Theatre on May 16, 1972, and for two months or more played along with *Ain't Supposed to Die a Natural Death*. Adapted from *The Party in Harlem*, another Van Peebles novel, *Don't Play Us Cheap* is a musical comedy with book, words, and music by Van Peebles; he also directed the Broadway production. Supposedly based on an actual experience the author had at a party in Harlem, the musical uses fantasy to present a story of demons that come to earth in the form of rats and cockroaches. These particular pests are anathema to denizens of urban communities and obviously were deliberately selected for their satirical potential and recognition by Blacks as demons that plague their lives. After assuming human form, two of the demons crash a Harlem house party, and one of the demons finds love with the young woman who lives in the house. The young woman's aunt, Miss Maybell, a Black mother figure who exudes warmth, strength, and an honest earthiness, also personifies wisdom and the will to survive. Nikki Giovanni said the show was the first by Van Peebles to present a message, although she cites this as a weakness in what was otherwise a natural, unpretentious interaction between characters who deal with each other on equal terms and confront the problems of life without bitterness or cynicism.[25] Clive Barnes must have detected the same theme as Giovanni, but he found reason to praise the show's universality and its concern that people learn "to be themselves, to avoid cant hyprocrisy and pretentiousness, and not only do their own thing, but even more to be their own thing."[26] Barnes also felt that Van Peebles might have served his show better had he brought in Gil Moses as director instead of directing the musical himself. In spite of many drawbacks Van Peebles might have caused the production by directing it himself, reviews for this show were much more favorable than those for *Ain't Supposed to Die a Natural Death*. Singled out for special praise were the veteran actors Esther Rolle as Miss Maybell and Avon Long as the demon Miss Maybell tries to seduce. Completing the cast were Thomas Anderson, Joshie Jo Armstead, Frank Carey, Robert Dunn, Rhetta Hughes, Joe Keyes, Jr., Mabel King, Geo. (Ooppee) McCurn, and Jay Vanleer.

The movie version of *Don't Play Us Cheap* was filmed in Santa Fe, New Mexico, with the same cast used in the Broadway production. Although the source of financing for the film is uncertain, it seems likely that it was Van Peebles' own production company, Yeah Inc., since he financed the stage show with profits from *Sweetback*. In fact, at one point he used his two Broadway shows to help push each other through various slumps. Using profits from one project to support another was a common practice of Van Peebles. With $70,000 earned from *Watermelon Man* and a loan of $30,000, he launched the production of *Sweetback*, and with earnings from *Sweetback* he produced *Don't Play Us Cheap*. Of course, he also invested heavily in *Ain't Supposed to Die a Natural Death* to keep it going until it found an audience. This willingness to use his own money is not typical of producers, but Van Peebles sees this as the only way to keep artistic and financial control. He states that his interest in writing and producing movies and plays is not motivated by desire to make money; rather, that the money he makes allows him to pursue his creative interests.

In both image and rhetoric, Van Peebles identifies himself with average working-class, grass-roots Blacks. It is this class and not the middle-class that Van Peebles calls his audience and to whom he directs his shows and films. Claiming that members of his audience don't read the popular White critics, he advertises in Black newspapers and over Black radio stations. This direct approach to the people helped him establish a communications network in the Black communities that created support for his shows and for other Black shows as well. He credits success in drawing this audience to keeping prices affordable, a lesson he learned in Chicago as a young man selling secondhand clothes to derelicts and winos.[27] Van Peebles' use of the provocative and sensational in subject matter and advertising has been criticized as unconscionable exploitation by both Blacks and Whites. No doubt to the chagrin of his critics, he points to his immense profits to justify his judgment in artistic and business matters. More importantly, he has been responsible for employing Blacks in all areas of film and theatre, from actors to technicians to business managers. Therefore, in the highly competitive and exclusive worlds of Hollywood and Broadway, perhaps Mel Gussow's assessment of Van Peebles is both accurate and deserved: "He is the first Black man in show business to beat the white man at his own game." [28]

During the late 1960s Charles Gordone got fed up with "rotten" plays and "rotten" directors, and he sat down to compose a letter to a friend but ended up writing *No Place to Be Somebody* (1969). Producer Richard Nash promptly turned it down, but Ashton Springer, a Black businessman who worked in Nash's office, read the script, liked it, and decided to produce it himself. When Springer was unable to raise seed money, the play found its way to Joseph Papp, who produced it Off-Broadway at the Public Theatre. *No Place to Be Somebody* was a success, and after it closed Off-Broadway, Springer got Papp's permission to transfer the production uptown. With Gordone's wife, Jeanne Warner, Ashton Springer formed Springer-Warner Production Company and for $20,000 moved the play to the ANTA, where it had another successful run and won the Pulitzer Prize for 1970. That, in essence, was how Ashton Springer got into producing for the theatre. He admits to having no previous desire to be a producer, although he had attended live theatre since he was fifteen. [29] He had been an ordinary businessman content with his life until *No Place to Be Somebody* started him on the road to another career.

Ashton Springer was born in Harlem in 1930. [30] Other than an aptitude for business and an appreciation for live theatre, nothing in his education or background prepared him to be a producer. Although he learned from *No Place to Be Somebody* that a producer doesn't necessarily have to have knowledge of producing, he felt he should get some training in theatre management if he was going to become seriously involved in theatre production. Through the help of a friend who owned a theatre, he was given the Vest Pocket Theatre in Detroit to operate.

Further training was received at the On Broadway in San Francisco. As producer of the road company production of Van Peebles' *Ain't Supposed to Die a Natural Death* he gained valuable knowledge and experience, especially in producing a musical. But before moving on to the lavish musicals that would bring him renown, Springer served as general manager for the play *My Sister, My Sister,* written by Ray Aranha and first presented in September 1973 at the Hartford Stage Company in Hartford, Connecticut. A haunting play that deals with the emotions of fear and guilt and the workings of the subconscious, *My Sister, My Sister* is reminiscent of the plays of Adrienne Kennedy. All the emotional and social stresses and strains, as well as the individual aberrations, of an entire Black family are revealed through the hallucinations and multiple personalities of a young woman named Sue Belle. Springer put together the New York production and opened it at the Little Theatre on April 30, 1974. As Sue Belle, Seret Scott won praise, but Springer learned how challenging it is to keep a play surviving on meagre resources.

Springer's production of the musical *Bubbling Brown Sugar* opened at the ANTA Theatre on March 2, 1976, and re-created the past both fictionally and literally. On the fictional level, the original idea of Rosetta LeNoire and book by Loften Mitchell concern three older Black performers who invite two young couples, one Black and the other White, to take a trip through Harlem of the 1920s, 1930s, and 1940s. The journey is only a pretext to revive and relive the cultural history of Black America. As a tribute to the Black musical heritage, the show features the music of greats such as Eubie Blake, Noble Sissle, Duke Ellington, Cab Calloway, and Billie Holiday. Included in the trip is a tour of famous Harlem nightspots, such as the Savoy, the Alhambra, and Small's Paradise. Famous landmarks like the Tree of Hope and the Pearly Gates are also covered. Legend has it that entertainers stood under the Tree of Hope for good luck, and newcomers to Harlem eagerly and excitedly passed through the Pearly Gates, an ironic euphemism for the subway entrance at 125th Street and Lennox Avenue. So while the basic storyline and incidents in the show are fictionalized, care is taken to make the music, lifestyles, names, and places completely authentic.

On a more literal level, the route which Ashton Springer and his associates took to reach Broadway with *Bubbling Brown Sugar* recalls that taken fifty-five years earlier by *Shuffle Along*. Both shows, by comparison, were bona fide hits on the road even before coming to New York. *Shuffle Along* had first to make a successful round of theatres in Washington, D.C., and Philadelphia. Likewise, *Bubbling Brown Sugar* played theatres in Washington and Philadelphia, but it also played in Chicago and Toronto before traveling back through Philadelphia and Washington enroute to New York. Although the show made money and earned a reputation on the road, the ten months spent touring was actually a test run to convince backers of its commercial survivability on Broadway. Further comparison reveals that *Bubbling Brown Sugar* and *Shuffle Along* were produced by producing teams. While *Shuffle Along* was produced by Miller, Lyles, Blake, and Sissle, the producers of *Bubbling Brown Sugar* were J. Lloyd Grant, Richard Bell, Robert Cooper, and Ashton Springer. The only White member of the team, Cooper, also directed the show. Grant and Bell had worked with Third World Cinema Productions, the company that produced the movies *Claudine*, with Diahann Carroll and James Earl Jones, and *Greased Lightning*, which starred Richard Pryor. Springer brought to the team his ability and experience as one of the few Black general managers in New York theater. The producers invested $30,000 of their own money to stage the first full production of *Bubbling Brown Sugar*. After the show amassed success on the road, the producers had no trouble in finding seven backers willing to invest the $400,000 needed to take the musical to Broadway.

Despite mixed reviews, *Bubbling Brown Sugar* found an enthusiastic audience. Most reviewers and critics agreed that the level of performance was outstanding, and practically all of them recognized the choreography of Billy Wilson. In the words of one critic: "This was his Broadway debut and he got the show moving magnificently, the best choreography to be seen currently on Broadway."[31] Receiving their share of accolades were veteran performers Joseph Attles and Avon Long. Also honored for their performances were Josephine Premice, Thelma Carpenter, Vivian Reed, and Barry Preston. Apparently, the

show succeeded as a musical revue rather than as a musical play
and depended heavily on recognized standards such as "Sophisticated Lady," "I Got It Bad," "Pray for the Lights to Go
Out," and "Sweet Georgia Brown." As a variety show with
minimal story, it worked, but as a musical, it was too seg-
mented and inharmonious. More importantly, it was becoming
apparent that Blacks would attend live theatre if more shows
were geared toward them. It was also being accepted universally that the time of the Black Broadway musical had again arrived, and whether or not this was a temporary fad, they were
attracting audiences and making profits. Concomitant with the
vogue for Black plays and musicals was the presence of the Black
producer determined to challenge traditional beliefs, policies, and
practices.

For the all-Black revamp of *Guys and Dolls*, Springer was associate producer to Moe Septee, who produced the show in association with Victor H. Potamkin. Directed and choreo-
graphed by Billy Wilson, the new version opened on July 21,
1976, at the Broadway Theatre. It was Wilson's idea to redo the
musical fable that depicts the lives of Broadway underworld
figures and the stalwart humanitarians who want to reform
them. The gamblers, hustlers, and Salvation Army missionar-
ies re-created for the stage by Abe Burrows and Jo Swerling were
based on characters created by Damon Runyon. The original all-
White version opened on Broadway November 20, 1950, and
ran for 1,200 performances. Although the characters and setting were distinctively ethnic White, they easily translated into
a Black idiom. Not uncommon to Black communities are small-
time gangsters, dance-hall girls, night clubs, storefront churches,
and illegal gambling. The biggest problem was making the musical recognizably Black without tampering with either the book
or the music and lyrics of Frank Loesser. Wilson's method was
to change the characters' way of speaking by allowing his actors to use their own speech patterns and to substitute Black
phrases for Jewish ones. He also invigorated the dance numbers with the lively "Black chic" that is found in Black nightclubs.[32] An obvious Black Church influence was responsible for
the spirited, revivalist rendition of "Sit Down, You're Rockin'

the Boat," a song that drew standing ovations and repeated encores when Ken Page (as Nicely-Nicely Johnson) sang it on Broadway.

Guys and Dolls was one of the biggest musicals on Broadway during the 1976 season. The show was helped by a one-minute television commercial made by the advertising agency of Blaine-Thompson Company, who began the trend with Pippin four years earlier. While Springer was obviously pleased with the commercial success of the show, he was more delighted by the opportunities it and Bubbling Brown Sugar gave talented Black performers. Other excellent performances in Guys and Dolls were contributed by Robert Guillaume as Nathan Detroit, the entrepreneur of the underworld; Norma Donaldson as his fiancée, Miss Adelaide; James Randolph as the gambler Sky Masterson; and Ernestine Jackson as Sister Sarah Brown, the Salvation Army ingenue in love with Masterson. Complementing these performers were Walter White as the menacing Big Jule; Emmett (Babe) Wallace as Arvide Abernathy, the Salvation Army militant; and Christophe Pierre as Benny Southstreet.

Not wanting to be limited, Springer took a chance with a fifty-nine-year-old operetta about airplane flying titled Going Up. Although the revival of this musical scored a triumph when it was presented by the Goodspeed Opera Company in East Haddam, Connecticut, it was an unlikely choice for a Black producer. Not only was it practically unknown, its theme and subject matter were somewhat anachronistic. Inspired by the 1903 maiden flight of the Wright brothers, playwright James Montgomery wrote a comedy titled The Aviator. In 1910 the play was staged unsuccessfully by Sam H. Harris and George M. Cohan. Ahead of its time, the play was benefited by the First World War and the interest it created in aviation. Consequently, in 1917 The Aviator was resuscitated and made into a musical with book and lyrics by Otto Harbach and music by Louis A. Hirsch.[33] The musical retained the comic flavor of The Aviator and tells the story of a young author named Robert Street who has written a best-selling book, also titled Going Up. In the book Street describes the exhilaration of flying although he himself has never flown in an airplane. Street is caught in his deception when, to win the affection of a young woman, he is challenged to an aerial duel by the young woman's fiancé, a French air ace. The Goodspeed production had an all-White cast, and Springer did not make any major changes when he moved the show to Broadway, where it opened on September 19, 1975. The musical either disappointed critics or aroused in them a warm feeling of nostalgia with "its smallness, its unpretentiousness." [34] However, the show did not interest enough people, and it closed after six weeks. The experiment cost Springer $47,000, but he was undismayed and encouraged Black producers to produce other than Black plays.

After conceiving the idea to turn *The Wonderful Wizard of Oz* into a Black musical, it took producer Ken Harper three years to locate investors. While Black musicals were scoring big on Broadway, some of them Black versions of previous, all-White productions, many potential backers doubted that theatregoers would accept the "Blackening" of a work so dear to White America. Ironically, the desire to do *The Wizard of Oz* in a new version was the only reason Harper wanted to become a theatrical producer. Born in 1939–40(?), he was reared in the Bronx, New York, and subsequently worked in radio and television, on which he had a bit part in the soap opera "Another World" for a year and a half. No doubt his eight years as a disc jockey and music director of a radio station helped him perceive the potential in a Black musical adaptation of the children's story written by Frank Baum and published in 1900. [35] Moreover, whereas Abe Burrows and Frank Loesser's widow oversaw the rehearsals of the Black *Guys and Dolls* to ensure that the book and music were not adulterated, Harper had freedom to shape *The Wizard of Oz* into a stylized rhythm and blues version. He began developing the project around a few songs written specially for the show by Charlie Smalls, and the only capital he had was his own savings and donations from family and friends. In all probability, the demonstrated success of other Black musicals on Broadway created a propitious climate, and Harper had few problems convincing Twentieth Century Fox to invest $650,000 in the show. But to this amount was added the expense of operating on the road to enhance the show's reputation and production quality, thus bringing the total amount to $1,165,000.

The Wiz, as the Black version was named, opened in New York on January 5, 1975, at the Majestic Theatre. Again, criticism was disparate, with most White critics being either unable or unwilling to resist a comparison with the movie that starred Judy Garland. "The little girl in the film played by Miss Garland was an utterly real person," stated a well-known critic for the *New York Times*, who added "The Dorothy in *The Wiz* never for a moment has those dimensions. And the Scarecrow, the Tinman and the Lion (who, in memory, must always be Bert Lahr), while fantastic, are merely amusing."[36] Reflecting the impressions of most Blacks who saw the show, Black reviewers interpreted it as a metaphor for the Black Experience and compared it to "a story about revival and restoration of human souls and human bodies, of disillusionment and hope, self-actualization and survival."[37] Whatever attitudes critics had, few if any could confess to not being moved by the show's originality and vitality. Geoffrey Holder directed the musical and designed the costumes, contributing an African and West Indian flair with bold designs and colors. George Faison's choreography was a mixture of balletic and modern-jazz exuberance. The book was by William F. Brown, who transformed Frank Baum's story into an urbanized epic that projected critical aspects of Black life and culture. Stephanie Mills starred in the role of Dorothy, with Hinton Battle as the Cowardly Lion and Tiger Haynes as the Tinman. In the role of the Wiz was Andre De Shields; Mabel King was cast as Evillene, the Wicked Witch; and Dee Dee Bridgewater played the part of the Good Witch Glenda.

During the 1974–75 theatrical season, *The Wiz* was nominated for eight Tony (Antoinette Perry) awards and received seven. Besides receiving the award for best musical of the season, the show garnered special honors for Geoffrey Holder as best director of a musical and best costume designer, Ted Ross as best supporting actor in a musical, Dee Dee Bridgewater as best supporting actress in a musical, Charlie Smalls for best score, and George Faison for choreography. The show ran for more than three years and grossed upwards of $18.5 million in ticket sales. Still, without the help it received at the outset from Melvin Van Peebles' grass-roots organization, the Wiz Group Sales, and Audelco, doubt looms that the show would have survived at all. Should that have happened, chances are that the film version, of which Ken Harper was executive producer, would never have come about.

During the Black Theatre revolution of the 1960s and 1970s, Black producers were primarily concerned with producing relevant Black plays and keeping artistic control in their own hands. Their goal, as stated, was not to treat Black Theatre as a business from which to profit financially. Black producers were united in their commitment to project a truer image of Black people through the theatrical medium, although such a commitment often dissuaded White producers and investors from backing Black shows. Even at the time when Blacks were making encouraging gains on Broadway and Off-Broadway, some leading theatre spokesmen were condemning the theory and practice of producing all-Black plays. Invariably, charges of racism were directed at the Black producers and seldom, if ever, at the White producer of the traditional all-White show. A *New York Times* article, "Casting by Race Can Be Touchy," illustrates this paradox:

The crucial question is whether a play should be cast entirely with Black performers or with a mixed company. The former can seem racist if there is no artistic validity for the switch in color. Then its only justification is to give minority actors employment. The mixed company makes far more sense. . . . In almost all cases, the healthiest approach is the integrated company.[38]

As it was, some Black producers seemed to share the sentiments of those critics who shunned the all-Black musical. However, by producing *Going Up*, an all-White show, Ashton Springer may have gone too far in the opposite direction and actually done little to eliminate the segregated Broadway musical and drama. On the other hand, Ken Harper's ambitions were to produce a musical based on a Japanese folktale and set in Japan. Using contemporary rhythm and blues and rock with a Japanese flavor, the musical was titled *Bamboo* and was to have a cast and staff comprised of Japanese-Americans, Puerto Ricans, Blacks, Whites, and any other nationalities who were best for the show. To his dismay, Harper found that the huge success of *The Wiz* was not advantageous 'in helping him attract backers to invest the $900,000 needed for the experimental musical. This time Twentieth Century Fox, which had suffered some losses on movie projects, could not be persuaded. At best, the experience was sobering and illuminated a reality that all Black producers recognized existed and that had to be addressed— the lack of Black investors. The only solution to this dilemma was the cultivation of Black investors who would encourage others to invest. Given the production costs on Broadway—$1.17 million for a musical and $270,000 for a straight play—investors were more likely to back a sure thing rather than take risks on a Black product that depended for its success on a heavy attendance by an uncertain Black audience.[39] The major problems faced by the Black producer, therefore, are those that have always plagued Blacks in the arts—economic inequality between Blacks and Whites, cultural bias, and the lack of a cultivated, sustained Black interest in art and theatre.

NOTES

1. Thomas D. Pawley, "The First Black Playwrights," *Black World*, April 1972,: p. 16.

2. Nathan Irvin Huggins, *Harlem Renaissance* (New York: Oxford University Press, 1971), p. 289.

3. James Weldon Johnson, *Black Manhattan* (New York: Arno Press and The New York Times, 1968), p. 204.

4. Loften Mitchell, *Black Drama* (New York: Hawthorn Books, 1967), pp. 191–97.

5. Peter Bailey, "Woodie King, Jr.: Renaissance Man of Black Theatre," *Black World*, April 1975, p. 6.

6. Biographical information on Woodie King, Jr., used in this section and sections that follow is based on material found in the following sources: Kalamu ya Salaam, "Making the Image Real: Black Producers of Theatre, Film and Television," *The Black Collegian*, March–April 1977, pp. 54–57; Woodie King, Jr., *Black Theatre: Present Condition* (New York: Publishing Center for Cultural Resources, 1981), pp. 78–81; Bailey, "Woodie King, Jr."; "*Black World* Interviews Woodie King, Jr.: Stage, Screen and Black Hegemony," *Black World*, April 1974, pp. 12–17.

7. Laura Ross, ed., *Theatre Profile 5* (New York: Theatre Communications Group, 1983), pp. 92–93.

8. Salaam, "Making the Image Real," p. 54.

9. Bailey, "Woodie King, Jr.," p. 4.

10. Ronald E. Kisner, "Rico Symbolizes Capitalistic System," *Jet Magazine*, 15 May 1975, pp. 20–22.

11. King, *Black Theatre: Present Condition*, pp. 72–77.

12. Maurice Peterson, "On the Road with the Wine-Sellers," *Essence*, November 1975, pp. 66–67, 84, 102, 106.

13. Salaam, "Making the Image Real," p. 57.

14. King, *Black Theatre: Present Condition*, p. 101.

15. "*Black World* Interviews Woodie King, Jr.", p. 13.

16. Biographical information on Melvin Van Peebles has been culled from the following works: Chester Higgins, "Meet the Man behind 'Sweetback,' " *Jet Magazine*, 1 July 1971, pp. 55–58; Joseph Horton, "Cable Car Pilots," *Sepia*, November 1972, pp. 25–28; Daniel J. Leab, *From Sambo to Superspade: The Black Experience in Motion Pictures* (Boston: Houghton Mifflin Co., 1973), pp. 242–49.

17. Leab, *From Sambo to Superspade*, p. 246.

18. Paul Carter Harrison, *The Drama of Nomo* (New York: Grove Press, 1972), p. 159.

19. Mel Gussow, "Baadasssss Success of Melvin Van Peebles," *New York Times Magazine*, 20 August 1972, pp. 10–11, 25–29.

20. *New York Times*, 31 December 1971, p. 12.

21. Eugenia Collier, "Ain't Supposed to Die a Natural Death," *Black World*, April 1972, pp. 80–81.

22. Maurice Peterson, "Ain't Supposed to Die a Natural Death," *Essence*, February 1972, p. 68.

23. Peter Bailey, "Annual Round-Up, Black Theater in America: New York," *Black World*, April 1972, pp. 32–33.

24. Clive Barnes, "Blacks Move through Gantlet of Slum," *New York Times* 21 October 1971, p. 55.

25. Nikki Giovanni, "I Get a Charge from Seeing Myself on Stage," *New York Times*, 28 May 1972, sec. 2, p. 1.

26. Clive Barnes, "Don't Play Us Cheap: Fun Comedy Musical," *New York Times*, 17 May 1972, p. 39.

27. Gussow, "Baadasssss Success," p. 26.

28. Ibid., p.10.

29. Jessica Harris, "Broadway's New Breed: Our Producers On the Great White Way," *Essence*, December 1977, p. 102.

30. For background information on Ashton Springer, the following sources were used: Curt Davis, "Springer-time on Broadway," *Encore American and Worldwide News*, 20 December 1976, pp. 30–31; Harris, "Broadway's New Breed," p. 102.

31. Clive Barnes, " 'Bubbling Brown Sugar' Boils at ANTA," *New York Times*, 3 March 1976, p. 30.

32. Judy Klemesrud, " 'Guys and Dolls' Comes Back Black," *New York Times*, 18 July 1976, sec. 2, p. 1.

33. Clive Barnes, "Goodspeed Company Presents Musical," *New York Times*, 30 June 1976, p. 22.

34. Mel Gussow, " 'Going Up' Is a Musical Charmer," *New York Times*, 20 September 1976, p. 39.

35. Background information on Ken Harper is based on the following sources: Harris, "Broadway's New Breed," pp. 105, 107; Maurice Peterson, "The Wiz's Wizzes," *Essence*, September 1975, pp. 53, 83–84.

36. Clive Barnes, "Black Musical Shows Vitality and Style," *New York Times*, 6 January 1975, p. 32.

37. Sharon Stockard Martin, "The Tanning Of Oz: Reflections on the Usurpation of a Myth," *Essence*, September 1975, pp. 32, 35.

38. Mel Gussow, "Casting by Race Can Be Touchy," *New York Times*, 1 August 1975, p. 1.

39. These figures are based on what it cost to produce a show on Broadway in 1978 and are taken from the following article: Tom Buckley, "The Big Bucks of Show Biz on Broadway," *Houston Chronicle*, 7 May 1978, p. 25.

5

A Chorus of Revolt

As late as 1920, there was no substantial body of plays by Black playwrights. This dismal reality motivated civil rights agencies and publications to address the problem, thus *Crisis* and *Opportunity* magazines tried to encourage Black playwrights by offering prizes for plays. By 1926 the situation was somewhat brighter, and W. E. B. Du Bois proclaimed, "There are available today a dozen or more plays of Negro life worth staging and the quantity and quality will increase very rapidly as the demand grows."[1] Although the number of Black plays and playwrights did increase, there was no corresponding demand for either. For the Black actor there continued to be opportunities to perform in the commercial theatre, but these were rare occasions in Black plays written by White playwrights. Willis Richardson's one-act play *A Chip Woman's Fortune* opened on Broadway in 1923, and Garland Anderson's *Appearances* followed in 1925, but neither had the impact to open a watershed of Black-authored drama. Contrarily, the same year Du Bois was applauding the increase in Black playwrights, David Belasco produced a hit on Broadway titled *Lula Belle*, a "sensational melodrama" that depicts the story of a beautiful Black girl's rise from the wanton streets of Harlem to a fashionable apartment in Paris. Co-authors of the play were Edward Sheldon and Charles MacArthur, two White playwrights. Produced also that same year was Paul Green's *In Abraham's Bosom*, which despite winning the Pulitizer Prize was still nothing more than a vehicle for melodramatic naturalism. But Émile Zola's sociological and literary theory, posited on the premise that an individual's character and fate are predetermined by his environment and heredity, found its most enthusiastic disciple in Eugene O'Neill. In plays such as *Emperor Jones* (1920) and *All God's Chillun Got Wings* (1924), O'Neill demonstrated that life uncovered and revealed in all its pretentious sordidness could be tolerated by a self-deluded White audience if the characters examined were Black and at a safe remove. Less experimental than the O'Neill plays but more blatantly stereotypical in its treatment of Blacks was Dorothy and DuBose Heyward's *Porgy* (1927).

A curious paradox of the 1920s is that the theories and concepts of intellectuals like Du Bois and Alain Locke seem to have had more in common with White playwrights. But Locke saw the rise in interest in native American folk drama per se as reason to feel encouraged about the possible development of a Black drama and Black theatre. He perceived the experimental explorations by White playwrights into Black themes, and the interest shown in them by both White and Black audiences, as a sign of a propitious breakthrough for the Black playwright. He observes:

Pioneering genius in the development of the native American drama, such as Eugene O'Neill, Ridgely Torrence, and Paul Green, now sees and recognizes the dramatically undeveloped potentialities of Negro life and folkways as a promising province of native idioms and source materials in which a developing national drama can find distinctive new themes, characteristic and typical situations, authentic atmosphere.[2]

At the same time, Locke realized that this theatrical interest in Black subject matter was due to a general interest in unexplored native American themes and was not fostered by a genuine concern for the well-being of Black people or for their achievements in the theatre. These are vital concerns Blacks had to accept for themselves.

Insisting that a viable Black drama and theatre must be consciously ethnocentric, Du Bois advised Black theatre groups not to produce plays by Shakespeare, Broadway renowns, and foreign White playwrights. Instead, he called for a Black drama developed in close collaboration between Black actor, playwright, and audience. Specifically, he stated:

The plays of a real Negro theatre must be: 1. *About us*. That is, they must have plots which reveal Negro life as it is. 2. *By us*. That is, they must be written by Negro authors who understand from birth and continual association just what it means to be a Negro today. 3. *For us*. That is, the theatre must cater primarily to Negro audiences and be supported and sustained by their entertainment and approval. 4. *Near us*. The theatre must be in a Negro neighborhood near the mass of ordinary Negro people.[3]

In his criteria Du Bois outlines a "folk-play movement" to be carried out by Blacks utilizing their own talent, industry, and economic resources. In terms of dramaturgy, Du Bois is less specific, saying only that the play must be a realistic depiction of Black life. The one-act play form was adopted by the majority of Black playwrights, however, since it is the best place to begin for someone who has had limited exposure to and experience in the theatre. Indeed, except for rare cases, the "serious" Black plays written before the 1920s were one-acters like Alice Dunbar-Nelson's 1918 *Mine Eyes Have Seen* and Mary Burrell's *They That Sit in Darkness* (1919). The three one-act plays selected by Du Bois' Krigwa Players to launch their 1926 "Negro Little Theatre Movement" were *Compromise* and *The Broken Banjo* by Willis Richardson and *The Church Fight* by Mrs. R. A. Gaines-Shelton. Interestingly, two of the plays were prize-winners in the *Crisis'* play contest, *The Broken Banjo*, a tradegy which took first prize in 1925, and *The Church Fight*, a comedy that placed second that year.

The concept of a Black folk drama, which was probably initiated by Ridgely Torrence's *Three Plays for a Negro Theatre*, was the source of much dispute and controversy. As interpreted by Black scholars and intellectuals, *folk* referred to the rural, southern Black of the soil, who because of his innocence and unpretentiousness best represented Black attitudes and responses toward life, religion, morality, and culture. To most Whites it obviously conjured up images of the exotic and erotic. From a contemporary perspective, a noted playwright and critic concludes: "While Torrence may have assisted in paving the way for the Negro to re-enter the downtown theatre, he also assisted in fathering a long line of neostereotype characters that ranged from the Emperor Jones to Abraham to Porgy to those of the present."[4] Nonetheless, the need to succeed commercially and at the same time depict Black people honestly and realistically was a dilemma not easily resolved by Black playwrights. Significantly, civil rights organizations such as the National Association for the Advancement of Colored People (NAACP) defined the Black playwright as a destroyer of negative Black images propagated through the entertainment media. Race propaganda plays, therefore, depicted educated, cultured, and high-achieving Blacks to offset the distorted, exaggerated stereotypes exploited for profit by both Whites and Blacks in the theatre. A prototype of this dramatic form is found in Angelina Weld Grimke's 1916 *Rachel*, a melodramatic polemic on the evil affects racial bigotry and violence have on a respectable, hard-working, middle-class Black family appropriately but sardonically named Loving. While this style of unadulterated racial propaganda did not become the playwriting norm in the 1920s, Black playwrights did not abandon protest altogether, but preferred to stick to the folk play in its various forms. Other representative plays of the period include *A Sunday Morning in the South* (1925) by Georgia Douglas Johnson, *Balo* (1924) by Jean Toomer, *'Cruiter* (1926) by John Matheus, and Willis Richardson's *The Idle Hand* (1929).

Although produced in 1929, Wallace Thurman's *Harlem* is indicative of the compromise playwrights of the 1930s often made between racial pride and commercial success—between the portrayal of Black people with depth and insight and the portrayal of popular, trite, and superficial characters and themes. In *Harlem* Thurman and White co-author William Rapp present a stark picture of the harmful effects Harlem life has on a Black family who migrated from the South. Praised for the honesty of his characterizations, Thurman was criticized for acquiescing to sensationalism by depicting scenes of gangland violence, sexual promiscuity, gambling, and numbers running. Theatre audiences still preferred Black caricatures to real-life characters in the 1930s, and the creation of the Federal Theatre project was a welcome opportunity for Black playwrights to explore serious Black subjects.

In 1930 Marc Connelly's *Green Pastures* opened on Broadway;

this theatrical spoof, which is supposed to be a sympathetic treatment of Black people, actually denigrates Black religion and culture. Hall Johnson and his choir appeared in the play, and perhaps to correct obvious distortions and to more accurately portray the psychological and cultural conflicts two contrasting modes of worship, African and Christian, can have on a religious people, Johnson wrote *Run, Little Chillun*. While upgrading the characters and subject matter to a more serious level, Johnson still included the spiritualized singing and praying that had stirred audiences who attended *Green Pastures*. Another Federal Theatre production of the era was Frank Wilson's *Brother Mose*, which was revived in 1934; it had appeared on Broadway in 1928 as *Meek Mose*. This production was followed in 1936 by another Wilson folk drama, *Walk Together Chillun*. Rudolph Fisher's *Conjur Man Dies*, also produced by the Federal Theatre in 1936, combines superstition with a detective story format. Independent of the Federal Theatre, Langston Hughes revived the emotional subject of miscegenation in *Mulatto*, which opened in October 1935 and became one of the longest-running plays by a Black playwright on Broadway. Hughes' *Don't You Want to Be Free?*, produced in 1938 by the Harlem Suitcase Theatre, is a pastiche of poetry, speeches, and songs experimental in form and theme; it set the tone for a more militant Black Theatre.

Condemned by reactionaries as too socialistic, the Federal Theatre was abolished by Congress in 1939, but Black theatre organizations quickly emerged to fill the vacuum. Both the American Negro Theatre (ANT) and the Negro Playwrights Company came into existence in 1940. Regrettably, the Negro Playwrights Company has the distinction of having produced only one play, *Big White Fog* by Theodore Ward (1940). First produced in 1938 by the Chicago unit of the Federal Theatre, Ward's play is set in the 1920s and depicts the travails of a Black family as they search for a means to liberation through Garveyism and Socialism. Heavily propagandistic, the play sides with Communism and espouses a belief in the unity and brotherhood of Blacks, Jews, and all poor, working-class peoples. ANT's first production was Abram Hill's *On Strivers Row*, a 1940 revival of the production staged a year earlier by the Rose McClendon Workshop Theatre. This is a satiric play that ridicules the pretentiousness of Black middle-class attitudes and values. *Natural Man* by Theodore Browne was the second production of ANT and was billed as a folk opera based on the life and exploits of the legendary "steel driving man," John Henry. In the play, produced in 1941, John Henry is cast as both victim of and rebel against racism and oppression. His cocky rebelliousness was overshadowed by the anger, defiance, and hostility of Bigger Thomas in the 1941 stage adaptation by Paul Green and Richard Wright of Wright's controversial, best-selling novel, *Native Son*. While blaming America's insensitivity toward minorities for Bigger's antisocial and violent behavior, *Native Son* is also weighted with socialist polemics. In terms of sound structure and dramaturgical flair, Theodore Ward's *Our Lan'* is recognized by many scholars and critics as the most accomplished play by a Black playwright up to the 1940s. Set in the time of Reconstruction, the play uses history, music, and pathos to give tragic but dignified dimensions to a newly freed slave named Joshuah Tain who leads a dedicated band of followers in an abortive armed struggle to claim land promised them by General Sherman at the end of the Civil War. *Our Lan'* opened in 1946 at the Henry Street Settlement Playhouse and was so successful it was moved to Broadway, where the power of its message failed to generate much enthusiasm.

Plays during the 1950s expressed a new form of protest, one that not only exhorted Black people to stand up for their rights but warned Whites that Blacks would settle for nothing less than their full share of the American Dream. Ironically, it seemed immaterial to angry Blacks—whether they were committed to non-violence or violence—that the American Dream was in a state of deterioration. Lorraine Hansberry's *A Raisin in the Sun* has been described as the quintessential integrationist play. However, the 1950s was an era of unprecedented Black unity and intolerance. While civil disobedience was the tactic accepted by the majority of Black activists, more aggressive and violent strategies were advocated by less tempered dissidents as well as debated vigorously in literature and drama. On the one hand were playwrights such as Hansberry who complained that Blacks had too long been denied the American

Dream; others argued that the Dream may not have been worth the sacrifices Blacks made in the two world wars.

A Medal for Willie by William Branch was produced in 1951 by the Committee for the Negro in the Arts, and it concerns the awarding of a medal to the family of a soldier who died fighting for his country. In open defiance, the soldier's mother castigates the military officials and hypocritical Whites in her southern hometown for believing that a medal could expiate the indignities her son suffered at the hands of his own countrymen. Branch's play *In Splendid Error* was produced in 1954 and takes up the question, Did Frederick Douglass regret repudiating John Brown's philosophy of violent revolution? Alice Childress' 1955 *Trouble in Mind* attacks White racist attitudes in the American theatre and ridicules that institution's recalcitrant acceptance of Black stereotypes. *A Land beyond the River* by Loften Mitchell (1957) is the story of a brave minister's fight to force school authorities in his South Carolina town to provide better educational facilities and opportunities to Black youngsters. The play is highlighted by a conflict between the minister, who favors non-violence, and a farmer, who advocates violence, over the use of armed aggression or the courts to settle their grievances. Louis Peterson's *Take a Giant Step* was a success on Broadway during the 1956–57 season. Critics hailed the play's universality and lauded Peterson's treatment of the problems faced by a Black boy who has grown up in a White neighborhood and who must now cope with his maturity and the changing racial attitudes of his former White friends. Still, among the plays of the 1950s, *A Raisin in the Sun* had the most influence on playwrights of the 1960s, many of whom adopted realism/naturalism to depict Black family life. But whether playwrights of the 1960s fell into the category of realism/naturalism, Marxism or structuralism, the prevailing mood of the period was that of revolt, outside and inside the theatre.

The debate over whether the 1960s did or did not witness a legitimate revolution is probably the result of conflicting definitions of revolution. There are the purists, such as Harold Cruse, who staunchly maintain that a clear-cut distinction exists between viable revolution and mere rebellion. Cruse clearly

articulates his point of view in the book *Rebellion or Revolution?*
He defines revolution as the unconditional overthrow of a system and the immediate replacement of that system with one
conceived by the revolutionaries. Random, undirected assault
upon a system by an organized group or groups is mere rebellion. Therefore, Cruse maintains that there never has been anything that can legitimately be called a Black Revolution in the
United States. He bases his argument upon Albert Camus' views
as emphatically stated in *The Rebel* and concludes: "The Black
Movement, which is a rebellion, has its 'revolutionary' limitations: It is a movement without any unique ideas of its own."[5]
He presents an intelligent and lucid discussion of the impact
and merits of a Black-led cultural revolution and explains:

Cultural Revolution means an ideological and organizational approach
to American social change by revolutionizing the administration, the
organization, the functioning, and the social purpose of the entire
American apparatus of cultural communication and placing it under
public ownership.[6]

Cruse's concept of revolution is based solidly on history. He
displays a salient respect for the scientific methodology em-
ployed by Marxism, with its emphasis on history. Revolution
is therefore defined in terms of the French Revolution, the Bol-
shevik Revolution, and Mao's Cultural Revolution. In other
words, revolution must be an all-out, philosophically inspired
military war against the existing social structure of a nation.
Cruse sees culture as forming merely one aspect of a social system, co-existing along with the economic system and the political system. In a highly industrialized society such as the United
States, culture can no longer be looked at in strictly anthropol-
ogical terms. Under advanced capitalism, culture becomes a
marketable commodity within the free enterprise system. As a
result, a cultural industry is produced. And, according to Cruse,
since America has never produced any culture of its own, it has
had to claim European "classical" culture and to exploit indigenous Black cultural achievements. Thus Cruse concludes that
Black Consciousness can be shaped into a theoretical frame-

work for viable revolution. But the primary purpose of the revolution, as fought on the cultural front, is to force shock waves through the nation. These shock waves should bring about a complete reordering within the nation's political, economic, cultural, and social structures. This cultural revolution should demonstratively change America.

As Ron Karenga sought to clarify in 1967, there were actually two revolutions under discussion. One was a revolution of consciousness, without which, explained Karenga, "we cannot wage the violent one."[7] It is clear from Karenga's manifesto (*The Quotable Karenga*) that he, too, fully understood the difference between a rebellion and a revolution. But he chose to explain revolution in terms of stages. His "bloodless revolution" would encompass the work necessary to elevate the level of consciousness within Black Americans. His "violent revolution" would consist of the war to bring about the collapse of the existing social and economic system in the United States. This rather ambiguous revolutionary ideology engendered Cruse's criticism. To him, these young radicals, full of idealism and imagination but lacking in historical and political insight, failed to give their revolutionary rhetoric sufficient theoretical clarity. Like Karenga and Baraka, Cruse feels that Blacks need to be made aware of their cultural identity before they can be organized into a cohesive revolutionary force. But there is clear disagreement between the two schools of thought. Karenga supports the idea that Blacks need to *create* a viable culture before they can realize their strength as a people. Baraka's pronouncements reveal these same sentiments. However, Cruse maintains that Blacks have already established a cultural identity in the United States; therefore, they need only to be convinced that they have just cause in order to be self-affirming rather than self-negating. This belief leads Cruse to express full support for Black Cultural Nationalism. Karenga and Baraka also advocate Black Nationalism. But the Black Nationalism they espouse is based on the concept of a separate nation. Cruse, at least, attempts to offer an original concept:

The political task of the Negro artist then, is to fight for the over-all democratization of the American apparatus of cultural communication

in order to make a place for the unrestricted expression of his own
ethnic personality, his own innate creative originality.[8]

Under the prevailing circumstances, Cruse obviously does not
feel that armed warfare is realistic.

But the Black Arts writers, who were the chief architects of
Black Revolutionary Drama, were inspired by the rhetoric and
actions of foreign revolutionaries and thinkers. These young,
militant artists and intellectuals bolstered their political indoc-
trination with the ideas of such revolutionary and Marxist stal-
warts as Amilcar Cabral, Kwame Nkrumah, Ho Chi Minh, Mao
Tse-tung, and W. E. B. Du Bois. The merger of these revolutionary ideas with the dramatic framework posed a dilemma for
Black playwrights who were products of American culture and
Western education. Revolutionary thinkers in Third World
countries were hostile to Western culture and condemned
Western literature as an "expression of bourgeois-intellectual
individualism."[9] Black Revolutionary playwrights, faced with
the problem of synthesizing a Black Aesthetic and an essentially Marxist political ideology, found it impossible to escape
fully the influence of what was perhaps the most successful attempt of the twentieth century to blend literary technique and
political ideology. It was, in other words, difficult to sidestep
completely the existential writers—especially Jean-Paul Sartre and
Camus. This point is highlighted whenever the concepts of
commitment and action are introduced.

It was Sartre who declared that an individual's life is void of
meaning and purpose if he has not committed himself to some
action. But Sartre does not necessarily concede that armed
struggle is superior action. He probably would have agreed that
if a person dies while engaged in a collective struggle, that person has the advantage of knowing that a part of him will continue to live through his action, which others will carry on.
During the Black rebellion of the 1960s and 1970s in the United
States, often referred to by Malcolm X as a bloodless revolution, the stages in the development of Black Consciousness were
sometimes delineated through the arts, especially poetry and
theatre.

Many of the Black Revolutionary plays of the sixties were

based on myth, but the myth of revolution the Black playwrights created was no less real than if it had actually taken place. Since theatre occurs in the mind, within the imagination of the spectators, the illusion of a revolution can affect the audience if its members are willing to accept the possibility of the real event. In most cases these plays were rituals and rites, designed for purposes of purgation and catharsis and intended, through stylized incantations, to will into reality an actual revolution. Yet this revolution could happen only if those needing the revolution were willing to take the necessary action to create one. The problem was one of identifying and imitating. Young militant playwrights modeled their rhetoric and style after that of revolutionaries in other countries fighting to liberate themselves from colonial and imperialistic oppression—revolutionaries who experienced real armed struggle, real bloodshed, the smell and taste of real dying. In the United States the revolution had to be experienced vicariously, to be fantasized, before it could be experienced in reality.

But, of course, the epoch did witness numerous violent riots and fiery rebellions that rocked American cities and alarmed the nation, while self-proclaimed young revolutionaries, close to two dozen of them members of the Black Panther Party, were martyred by the police. Some believed the seriousness and ardor with which the Federal Bureau of Investigation and local police forces undertook their missions of eliminating the threat of "anarchy" exposed their eagerness to become participants in a real-life drama being played in the streets.

The first revolutionary poems and plays, then, were more or less in anticipation of the mounting ferment of the times. Black Revolutionary Theatre set an example for similarly styled theatres to follow—El Teatro Campesino, the San Francisco Mime Troupe, and the Guerrilla Theatre. All had as their primary purpose the development and promulgation of propaganda. Amiri Baraka, precursor of the trend, confined his early revolutionary works to the stage, but later he too moved onto the streets. The Black Revolutionary Theatre characteristically went further than the mere protest engaged in by the other revolutionary theatre. The Black Revolutionary Theatre called explicitly for armed struggle. The Black Revolutionary plays were, in effect, advertisements for guerilla warfare, yet curiously these plays drew heavily upon Aristotelian-style pathos. Baraka and his group were intent upon affecting the characters and personalities of those persons in the audience by rousing basic emotions such as pity and fear.

The intention of seemingly brutal and nihilistic plays such as Jimmy Garrett's *We Own the Night*, in which a would-be urban guerilla fighter kills his reactionary mother, is to promote the idea that revolutionaries should be depicted as heroes. Three other plays that are steeped heavily in the revolutionary mystique are *We Righteous Bombers*, *Black Terror*, and *Sister Son/ji*. Richard Wesley wrote *Black Terror*, and Sonia Sanchez is the author of *Sister Son/ji*, but there has always been some question as to the exact author of *We Righteous Bombers*. The credited playwright is Kingsley B. Bass, Jr., reported to have been a twenty-four-year-old Black man killed by the police during the Detroit uprising. It has been long speculated, though, that the play was actually written by Ed Bullins, even though his long plays were written in the mode of realism or naturalism, while the expressionistic *We Righteous Bombers* turns out to be a pastiche of futuristic fantasy and science fiction. Overall, the playwright appears to be attempting a complex experiment. The play itself is not original. It is actually an unabashed reworking of Albert Camus' *The Just Assassins*—which itself is an adaptation of Boris Savinkov's *Souvenirs d'un terroriste*. In *We Righteous Bombers* characters are renamed but many passages are lifted whole from the original. Camus in his play was exploring the philosophical idea that there are limitations to action. In other words, he asked the question of whether revolutionaries and terrorists who proclaim themselves defenders of justice have the moral right to take justice into their own hands and kill in the name of an ideal. *We Righteous Bombers* continues this debate with questionable success.

It could be that the author of *We Righteous Bombers* has misunderstood Camus' intentions in *The Just Assassins*. Camus did not see revolutionary and/or terrorist actions as presenting an absurd problem, but he did realize that such actions presented serious moral and ethical questions that obviously have to be worked out by revolutionaries and terrorists who claim justice for people who are being punished unjustly. A contradiction exists when the terrorists are convinced that the achievement of their objectives does not offer vindication to those members of the oppressive group who may be innocent. Camus' position is that terrorists do have a moral responsibility to preserve the lives of innocent people, even though this responsibility may impede the successful completion of their goals. The author of *We Righteous Bombers* seems to be trying to stretch the theme so that the contradiction, instead of being a moral dilemma, is one that warrants senseless brutality. Unfortunately, in trying to bring this switch off, the playwright uses certain contrived scenes and incidents and destroys any credibility the play might either have on its own or have inherited from its predecessor. *We Righteous Bombers* turns out to be, more than anything else, paranoid and fatalistic.

Richard Wesley's *Black Terror* is another improvisational turn upon *The Just Assassins*. Although the play takes up the question of the limitations of action, it goes a step further by attacking the fatalism and suicidal zeal inherent in the philosophy directing such European terrorist groups as those depicted in *The Just Assassins*. The play's dialectic evolves from two philosophical points of view; more specifically, it presents a dramatic critique on the dialectics of Black thought in the United States. Invariably, all these philosophies are concerned with attitudes toward the oppression of human beings and the most realistic and effective strategy for dealing with that oppression. However, such overriding emphasis on a single question is neither a paranoid obsession nor merely the product of an impoverished imagination. Rather, the question is of universal importance in that the majority of the world's peoples are living under some form of oppression. The playwright wanted to depict "certain ideologies" that were directing the Black rebellion of the 1960s in the hope that Black people would be able to weigh the pros and cons of all sides and come to a decision as to which course of action seemed the most appropriate. What especially concerned Wesley was the nihilistic attitude of "revolutionary suicide" that was shaping the course of action for many Blacks during the political climate of 1969–70.

In light of now historic events, the Black Revolutionary Theatre of the 1960s and 1970s may have failed to bring about the collapse of the existing American system, or to alter radically the cultural perception of the American populace. But this failure does not mean that the concepts and intellectual bases that provided a foundation for the movement were aborted. Indeed, quite the contrary is true; therefore, the latest attempt by the most influential member of the Black Arts/Theatre Movement, Amiri Baraka, to adopt the forms of epic theatre and "socialist agit-prop" as means of voicing his conversion to "Marxism–Leninism–Mao Tse-tung Thought" demands serious attention. With the production and publication of the plays *The Motion of History* (1975–76) and *S–1* (1976), Baraka's espousal of Marxism-Leninism is firmly established, yet it must be understood that although Baraka has retailored his rhetoric, his stand on the subject of revolution is just as firm. Curiously, Harold Cruse had accused Baraka of lacking an effective critique, necessary not only for the development of a successful nationalistic movement but for a revolution as well, so these plays could be in response to critics such as Cruse. Still, this new phase in Baraka's strategy can readily be viewed as a natural evolutionary process. The playwright himself explains, "And we have tried to move from petty bourgeois radicalism, nationalism (and its low point of bourgeois cultural nationalism) on through to finally grasping the science of revolution, Marxism–Leninism–Mao Tse-tung Thought."[10] Nevertheless, the fact remains that there are two more plays to be added to Baraka's still-expanding oeuvre, and a look at them may give insight into the direction Black Revolutionary Theatre might take in the future.

The Motion of History is written in the epic style. Totalling four acts and fifty-one scenes, it is didactic and propagandistic in concert with the intentions and purposes of the playwright; a multitude of characters, most of them important historical figures, are used in the play. The scenes are short and move rapidly; means of distancing are obvious, apparently to force the objective participation of the audience. Baraka's purpose is to use history—by connecting and contrasting historical events—as a means of analyzing the American system, its origin and development, its present condition, and its future. Two men, one White (Richie Morarity) and the other Black (Lenny

Nichols), provide the nexus of the multifarious scenes and incidents. The play's intentions are manifested through these two men. Intermittently, between scenes of historical events, Morarity and Nichols are seen evolving an expanded consciousness as they acquire a clear view of present realities through historical analysis. As typical bourgeois reactionaries—Nichols striving to reach the top as a Black professional, Morarity living the life of a hip existentialist—they soon realize that real purpose and liberation mean the replacement of monopoly capitalism by the "dictatorship of the proletariat." This accomplishment, they know full well, cannot be brought about without a revolution, and the revolution must involve a unification of the entire working-class with all oppressed nationalities. The job, then, for Morarity and Nichols is to organize these forces into an effective political party, the Marxist-Leninist party.

S–1 was a Senate bill that, if passed, would permit the federal government to deter any form of dissidence aimed against the American power structure. The S–1 bill would, in essence, legalize a form of fascism. It calls for the death penalty to be automatically imposed for certain crimes of sedition. The bill also mandates that astronomical fines upwards of $100,000 and three to seven years in prison or death be imposed against anyone possessing government "secret information." It legalizes wiretapping without court approval, and while imposing harsh sentences on "criminal dissidents," waives prosecution of public officials "who act illegally on orders." The clear intention of the S–1 bill, besides legalizing fascism and making preparations for a war with Russia, is to eradicate completely the revolutionaries in the United States.

The play itself revolves around S–1. Scenes are presented showing the bill being debated, voted on, and eventually approved by Congress and upheld by the Supreme Court. Two revolutionary heroes emerge, Lawrence ("Red") Hall and his wife and comrade-in-arms, Lillian ("Lil") Hall. The process of evolving from reactionary bourgeois to reborn Marxist-Leninist is represented by news reporter Walt Stevens. Parts of the basic format for *The Motion of History* are repeated, especially the projection of scenes from history to demonstrate the commonality between exploited Whites and other oppressed minorities. Baraka is particularly concerned with exposing racism as a strategy of the capitalists to divide the working-classes along superficial racial lines, thus preventing their unification and ensuring the continued existence of the capitalist system.

Clearly this is a time when some intellectuals feel it is their responsibility to align themselves with the masses. This attitude is more evident in the European countries. Before his death Jean-Paul Sartre had come out in favor of Marxism and in support of the commitment by intellectuals to the common people. And certainly it cannot be denied that Socialism and Communism are establishing themselves as moving forces in the world. But America is a peculiar place, as Baraka knows; and racism, nurtured over centuries, is still a hard, everyday reality. Forming a coalition between all working-class Whites and minorities in the United States for purposes of revolution is seen as a formidable task. It seems more realistic and practical—and original—for Black or White activists to follow Richard Wright's advice and use Marx as the skeleton on which to construct a wholly unique and relevant critique.

Undeniably, the Black Revolutionary Theatre was primarily didactic and geared toward arousing Black people to take aggressive action to change the state of their existence in the United States. Since plays in this theatre were written exclusively for a Black audience unaccustomed to attending live theatre, it was necessary for Black Revolutionary playwrights to innovate dramatic forms. Most of these playwrights, since they were new at writing, merely adapted the one-act play form, and the one-act play was well suited to a theatre whose objective was to deliver a message and to describe a course of action. The language used by these playwrights varied between the contrived poetic diction of *Madheart* and *Sister Son/ji* to the prose dialogue of *We Righteous Bombers* and *Black Terror*. But the formula for Black Revolutionary Theatre is simple: Blacks are the protagonists, victims, and classical heroes, while Whites are the antagonists, oppressors, and major hostile forces destructive to Black aspirations. Explicit examples of this formula are found in Bullins' *The Gentleman Caller* and Baraka's *Experimental Death Unit #1*, where the quest for Black heroism is reduced to a simple matter of executing exploitative Whites. The concept is extended in Baraka's *Black Mass,* in which the symbolic White beast is the personification of all evil existing in the world. Nonetheless, the Black Revolutionary Theatre is distinguished by its daring experimentation.

But by no means was the Black rebellion in America composed of only one philosophy and prescriptive of only one course of action, nor was the push for social and political change exclusively Black. But much of the inspiration and creativity of the rebellion of the 1960s was the contribution of those individuals who had experienced social, political, economic, and cultural repression firsthand. Such repression, although the most important element of the Black Experience, does not constitute the entire phenomenon. It is composed—like human existence—of a multiplicity of experiences. Therefore, in attempting to redefine, clarify, and restore to Blacks an awareness and appreciation of their "being," Black artists used not only activist strategies but also phenomenological techniques. In a real sense, writers such as Baraka, Bullins, Milner, and Caldwell attempted to do for Blacks what such writers as Edmund Husserl, Karl Jaspers, and Sartre attempted to do for Europeans. Simply, that was to describe to modern man, in a way he could comprehend and actually visualize or sense, what it means to be alive and vital in the universe. It boils down to the axiom "I am, therefore I think; and because I think I can perceive a purpose for taking meaningful action." Therefore, the development of Black Consciousness—the rediscovery of self and the need to take positive action to achieve, first, individual freedom, then collective freedom—involves a series of steps, or stages. These are (1) accusation and condemnation, followed by (2) awareness and acceptance, (3) commitment, and (4) action.

Taken as a whole, the Black Theatre of Revolt reflects, in some way, the four basic steps in the development of Black Consciousness. But playwrights heard as the chorus of revolt were individual writers as well. Not always are all of these steps contained in any one work. And even when one or more do appear within a play, not always are they graphically presented. The search for consistency and uniformity has caused many critics to misinterpret and misrepresent the movement. Early reviewers and critics, such as Henry Hewes in his review of *Happy Ending* and *Day of Absence* in the *Saturday Review* for June 26, 1966, and David Littlejohn in his *White on Black*, tended to reduce Black plays of revolt to simplistic statements of resentment and anti-White bias. Baraka's plays especially came under sharp attack; *The Toilet* elicited this criticism from a noted critic: "*The Toilet* is a barely stageable homosexual fantasy in which the setting is a urinal and the theme the sexual nature of violence and the degradation of the white world."[11] Critics seemed aware that the plays were a radical departure from accepted bourgeois theatre, as well as a step beyond the social-protest plays of the 1930s, still they generally believed that these plays had no more to commend themselves than a deep-seated hatred for Whites. Even a somewhat indecisive play like Douglas Turner Ward's *Day of Absence* was seen by Hewes to be an example of an anti-White theatre of resentment. And plays such as Baraka's *Jello* and *Madheart*, as well as Bullins' *How Do You Do?* continued to garner such criticism while pursuing the case for Black Consciousness.

Charles Gordone emerged as the voice of those opposed to the basic tenet of the Black Theatre Movement—that the Black Experience is a singular and unique phenomenon. To Gordone, the Black Experience is only one aspect of the total American experience. He reasons that without the presence of the White experience, there could be no Black Experience, and vice versa. The two are dynamically interrelated, each determining the individual uniqueness of the other. America's greatest social problem is the color problem. The Black-White symbiosis can only be satisfactorily achieved through the cooperation of all parties concerned. Gordone is thus suspicious of any radical political movement that might further divide the races.[12]

Equally important, though, is the nonpolitical way Gordone perceives the theatre. The theatre, he maintains, should depict life, since the image of life is what makes it universal. Once the social problems these plays depict have been settled, their significance for posterity will be determined by the insight with which they portrayed life apart from the social and political issues of the day. The Black Theatre Movement is too much conditioned by contemporary politics. Of course, he is not alone in his belief that there should be a separation of polemics and art.

Ralph Ellison also agrees.[13] Still, Gordone wants it understood
he is not trying to escape reality or responsibility:

I have political views, but I'm not politically bent. In other words, I
don't want to write something that is supposed to propagandize, or
have any kind of polemics, any overt polemics. . . . I just want to
talk about people.[14]

Nonetheless, when Charles Gordone's *No Place to Be Somebody* won a 1970 Pulitzer Prize, the work was lauded by reviewers and critics as the most accomplished play within the "new"
Black Theatre. Despite the author's protests, the White reviewers (due to a lack of depth or a natural tendency to stereotype)
compared the play to the works of Baraka and Bullins and
viewed it as another polemic on Black Power. In the words of
one critic:

Directed by Ted Cornell at the small arena-type Other Stage . . . the
production is, among other things, a showcase for two wonderful performances, by Ron O'Neal as Gabe Gabriel, the inside-and-outside-the-
play observer, and by Nathan George as Johnny Williams, the saloon-
keeper clenched with every conceivable Black hatred against "Charlie." Indeed, it is "Charlie fever" that is Gordone's central theme, the
anti-white fever that every Black must pass *through* if he is to achieve
self and society.[15]

These comments suggest that White critics are often guilty of
making hasty generalizations about Black Theatre and are determined to evaluate all Black playwrights by one criterion. Irony
is seen in such denunciations as Gordone's, for obviously any
dramatic treatment of the Black Experience by Black playwrights will automatically be classified by the critics as Black
Theatre.

Gordone has said of *No Place to Be Somebody*, "It's a comedy,
but it has tragic overtones." In all fairness to the playwright,
the play is not just another racial diatribe. In fact, the black humor in *The Blacks* and *No Place* is based on metaphysical incongruity. To achieve this feeling of metaphysical incongruity, black
humorists go beyond satire with its use of exaggeration and wit
by adding contradiction and irony. Genet's Blacks, for in-

stance, are revolutionaries waging war against the White power structure they aspire to replace in all its grandiose dress and absurd customs. Genet sees the oppressed becoming oppressor as a vicious cycle and a metaphysical incongruity. Although *black humor* is a term coined in the 1960s, the style can be discerned in Shakespeare. *Troilus and Cressida*, for example, views the world as a "grim farce." In this particular play, Shakespeare shows that what man believes to be his great accomplishments are inconsequential in the infinite and indifferent universe. The black humor of *No Place to Be Somebody* is created by the tension between the characters' station in life and their aspirations. Gordone is not a determinist; in their desperate quest to "become somebody," his main characters have set their ambitions in excess of their immediate limitations. Central character Johnny Williams heads the list of characters suffering the malaise of metaphysical incongruity, and his burning ambition to become a syndicate boss finally consumes him.

Both Baraka and Bullins are prolific playwrights, but Bullins is perhaps the more versatile. In fact, his eclecticism typifies the variegated trends and styles exemplified by the Black Theatre Movement; these styles range from naturalism to fantasy to surrealism, and sometimes to the sinister and macabre. Although these playwrights experiment, they do not experiment merely for the sake of experimentation. Their practice is to select an appropriate form or style to fit a particular mood or experience, and/or philosophic idea. More precisely, a Black aesthetic/political approach to playwriting places more emphasis on subject matter than on style and form and attacks traditional attitudes, customs, and beliefs of Blacks by advocating a Black value system. Conventional literary styles are either abandoned completely, modified, or integrated. Bullins explains:

In this manner the play could begin naturalistically with a character in a realistic setting and progress through expressionism, surrealism, absurdity and back to realism, dramatizing the journey of the character through his own psyche to reach his loss of innocence, self-awareness or illumination.[16]

This approach typifies a Marxist view toward literature by forming "equitable views by stirring up contradictions within the spectator's mind, and [trying] to forge accurate intellectual concepts from the dynamic clash of opposing passions."[17]

A breakdown of Bullins' works into categories can also sum up the variety of forms and styles utilized by other playwrights in the movement. Such a design might reflect the following:

I. School
   1. Realistic/Naturalistic
      A. *Théâtre Verité* (a term used to demonstrate certain theatrical characteristics that parallel those of *cinema verité*)
   2. Revolutionary/Nationalistic
      A. Guerilla Theatre
      B. Street Theatre
      C. Black Revolutionary Theatre
II. Form/Genre
   1. Satire
   2. Tragi-fantasy
   3. Improvisational/Extemporaneous
   4. Happenings
   5. Recitations
   6. Screenplays

Bullins' plays within the Realistic/Naturalistic category have generated the most attention and criticism. Practically all of the full-length plays fall, in one way or another, into this category. Also, it appears he has selected this style for his Twentieth Century Cycle, which so far includes *The Corner, Goin' a Buffalo, In the Wine Time, In New England Winter, The Duplex, The Fabulous Miss Marie,* and *The Taking of Miss Janie.*[18]

The Corner presents the recurring character Cliff Dawson in pencil sketch and also provides sketches of basic themes and motifs that, like certain characters, are more fully developed in the longer plays. Furthermore, Bullins achieves dramatic impact with the street-corner setting, which becomes a microcosmic society, a veritable subculture and a milieu of intense social congress. In overcrowded American cities the street corner not only provides a convenient meeting place but functions in a way similar to the traditional Black Church E. Franklin Frazier describes as an "invisible institution." Consequently, the street corner can be, and often is, an alternative world for marginal types. Because these confined streets are hostile and perilous, only the most hardened cynics find acceptance and success there. And these outcasts and "outlaws" serve as a warning to those who aspire to greater accomplishments within the elusive system. "Good boys" and "good girls" do not "hang" on the corner, but spend their idle time in church or home studying. To be seen hanging on the corner means that one has transgressed and is psychologically and spiritually lost. But by turning his or her back on the corner and breaking the weak bonds of friendship that exist there, the individual has, at least symbolically, taken the first step toward "salvation." Giving up the corner is tantamount to beginning a new life. In *The Corner* the character Cliff Dawson demonstrates such a renunciation:

Bummie: Cliff . . . is there anything bothering you, man?

Cliff (annoyed): Awwww . . . man . . . it's just one of those goddam days, I guess.

Bummie: But Somethin' had to happen, man. This ain't like you, Cliff.

Cliff: What's like me, huh? To be a bum? To drink wine and fuck bitches in junky cars? To stand half the night on some street corner that any fucken cop can come up and claim? Is that like me?

Bummie: But, man, we've always done it. Even before you went into the Navy and got out.

Cliff: But I ain't doin' it no more, Bummie . . . no more.

Bummie: Are you goin' away, man?

Cliff: Nawh . . . nawh . . . not goin' away no more. Not anymore . . . I'll be here for a long time, man. I'm a family man now.

Bummie: You and Lou are gonna get hitched?

Cliff: Hitched? Hummp . . . that's funny . . . I never thought about that.

Bummie: You gonna settle down, man?

Cliff: Yeah, Bummie, yeah. Lou's gonna have a baby. I'm gonna be a father.

Bummie: Well . . . I'll be damned.

Cliff: Yeah . . . you can start callin' me Daddy Cliff.

Bummie: Hey . . . man . . . that's great. C'mon up on "the avenue" . . . I'll buy you a drink.

Cliff: Nawh, man. I'm not up to it. I'm goin' in.

Bummie: Hey, man, you changin' already.

Cliff: Yeah, maybe I am. Well, I'll see ya, man. (*Cliff* exits.)[19]

Plays such as Bullins' that explicitly depict Black street life have their share of detractors. Criticism of the plays is leveled at both their form and content. Bullins has been accused of shunning conventional dramaturgy, and of abandoning form altogether. Reviewing *The Duplex*, Walter Kerr writes: "[It] is not intended as a 'white,' neatly tooled, traditionally well-made play but as a play derived wholly—in form and in feeling—from Blackness."[20] On the other hand, Hazel Bryant sees a danger in the tendency to venerate street people while denigrating middle-class values. She warns:

We put down the church; we put down the middle-class; we put down women. We've alienated these people even before we got them by putting them down. We have not found support in the Black community except among the Black avant-garde, which is not a very large class and even their interest is not financially supportive. . . . Let's face it, our people will not support anything but the best.[21]

Theatre professionals, however, are not the only critics of certain trends and styles promoted as Black Theatre by playwrights and producers. Responding to the musicals of Melvin Van Peebles, an offended theatre consumer protests:

In the theatre I have seen Blacks in the ghetto, in oppression and being humiliated by the society we live in. I have also watched the theatre slowly evolve into romanticizing the pimp, the dope addict, the prostitute and the almighty Black stud. You are constantly showing us as "freaks of nature." . . . By doing this, Blacks in control of the arts are being as racist as the white man they hate so much for having done it to them for so many years. We Blacks who are proud to be Black inside our souls do not think it is so wonderful to see those Blacks who have been unfortunate being glorified.[22]

There were playwrights who sought to offset negative aspects by projecting more positive concepts of Black life. These playwrights usually adopted (and adapted) the style of realism/naturalism to depict the crises, challenges, failures, and sometimes triumphs of the Black family. Five plays that have been mentioned elsewhere in this study serve best to illlustrate this particular approach.

In *Ceremonies in Dark Old Men* Lonne Elder III uses melodrama and realism to relate the story of a Harlem family headed by a widower who barely makes a living as a barber. Russell Parker fears seeing his sons lured into easy, but destructive, lives of crime. Already, his daughter, who practically supports the household, is in danger of losing her femininity to disillusionment and bitterness. And because Mr. Parker himself feels impotent and vulnerable as a man and father, he is fearful of losing his own sense of manhood and self-respect. A similar situation is found in Milner's *Who's Got His Own*. The funeral of a deceased father is the occasion for a bereaved widow, son, and daughter to undergo emotional catharsis, in which the dead father's children reveal depths of resentment and shame at the way he humbly capitulated to racism to make a living for his family. Loften Mitchell felt Milner was stating "that nothing in America has changed in terms of the Black Experience."[23] Joseph Walker's *The River Niger* praises both the often maligned Black father and the ancient civilizations of Black Africa, of which the play's central character, Johnny Williams, is immensely proud. Johnny Williams is portrayed as a hard-working, harddrinking house painter/postal worker with a poetic temperament who sacrifices his life not only to protect his own family but to save a gang of Black youths engaged in an aborted revolutionary cause. Although Phillip Hayes Dean's *The Sty of the Blind Pig* is set in the 1950s at the height of the Civil Rights Movement, it treats the timeless subject of emotional and spiritual alienation. In this case Alberta is alienated emotionally and spiritually from her domineering mother and from society. Approaching middle age, Alberta has denied herself while unselfishly serving others, including her mother, her church, and the White family for whom she works. Even a brief romantic tryst, while her mother is absent from the house, with a blind blues singer fails to liberate Alberta from the demands of others; the play seems to reinforce the idea that strength to endure resides in the Black woman. Leslie Lee's *The First Breeze of Summer* is about a Black family and its matriarch, a woman who in her youth was deceived by men, two Black and one White. In the play, Gremmar, on the eve of her demise, recalls the past and how she was forced to be deceitful and endure humiliation and poverty to keep her children together as a family. Overall, one could say that these plays, while projecting a positive concept, did not always depict positive characters.

Since the Black Theatre Movement of the 1960s and 1970s attempted to utilize artistic means to achieve social and political ends, new and innovative theatre styles and forms were needed to develop this radical theatre. Thus, leading spokesmen for the movement advocated the development of a Black Aesthetic based on Black cultural forms and the Afro-American oral tradition. A question arises: Why should it be necessary to create a Black Aesthetic when it is obvious that one already exists? This dilemma in which Black playwrights found themselves is one that still has not been resolved. Black playwrights merely adopted any form that could convey a message and bring about change.

NOTES

1. W. E. B. Du Bois, " 'Krigwa Players Little Negro Theatre': The Story of a Little Theatre Movement," Crisis, July 1926, p. 134.

2. Alain Locke, "Introduction: The Drama of Negro Life," in Plays of Negro Life: A Source Book of Native American Drama, eds. Alain Locke and Montgomery Gregory (Westport, Conn.: Negro Universities Press, 1970), p. xiii.

3. Du Bois, " 'Krigwa Players Little Negro Theatre,' " p. 134.

4. Loften Mitchell, Black Drama: The Story of the American Negro in Theatre (New York: Hawthorn Books, 1967), p. 69.

5. Harold Cruse, Rebellion or Revolution? (New York: William Morrow and Co., 1969), p. 109.

6. Ibid., p. 124.

7. Maulana Ron Karenga, "From the Quotable Karenga," in The Black Power Revolt: A Collection of Essays, ed. Floyd B. Barbour (New York: Collier Books, 1968), p. 195.

8. Cruse, Rebellion or Revolution? p. 124.

9. V. I. Lenin, On Literature and Art (Moscow: Progress Publishers, 1978), p. 26.

10. Amiri Baraka, The Motion of History and Other Plays (New York: William Morrow and Co., 1978), pp. 13–14.

11. C. W. E. Bigsby, *Confrontation and Commitment: A Study of Contemporary American Drama, 1959–1966* (Columbia: The University of Missouri Press, 1968), p. 142.

12. Charles Gordone, *The Black Experience in the Arts*, a filmstrip produced and edited by Lilla Brownstone (Pleasantville, N.Y.: Warren Schloat Productions).

13. Addison Gayle, Jr., ed., *The Black Aesthetic* (New York: Doubleday/Anchor Books, 1971), p. 38.

14. Gordone, *Black Experience*, p. 15.

15. Jack Kroll, "Real Black Power," *Newsweek*, 2 June 1969, p. 101.

16. Gordone, *Black Experience*, p. 14.

17. Sergei Eisenstein, *Film Form* (New York: Harcourt, Brace and World/A Harvest Book, 1949), p. 47.

18. Plays listed here have been determined on the basis of those in print or reported to have been produced. More than these may have already been completed, produced, and/or published, but at this time I am unaware of them.

19. Ed Bullins, *The Theme Is Blackness: The Corner and Other Plays* (New York: William Morrow and Co., 1973).

20. Walter Kerr, "Mr. Bullins Is Himself at Fault," *New York Times*, 19 March 1972, sec. D, p. 1.

21. McCandlish Phillips, "Message of Street Theatre Is Strong," *New York Times*, 22 June 1971, p. 28.

22. Marshall Hill, "Melvin Van Peebles—A Black Exploiter?" letter to the editor, *New York Times Magazine*, 10 September 1972, p. 33.

23. Mitchell, *Black Drama*, p. 223.

6

Other Black Playwrights: The
Non-Polemical Structuralists

A few Black playwrights, such as Charles Gordone, were able to capitalize on the interest created by the Black Arts Movement while remaining unaligned with it, but others who opted for complete freedom of expression received almost none of the attention they deserved. Two of the most unique and original Black playwrights at the periphery of the Black Theatre Movement were Adrienne Kennedy and Edgar White. The differences between the independent playwrights (Gordone, Kennedy, and White) and the aligned playwrights are not great. Baraka and Bullins are just as daring and experimental as Kennedy and White. *Black Mass, Slaveship,* and *The Electronic Nigger* are among the best avant-garde dramas of the 1950s and 1960s, as are the plays of Adrienne Kennedy and Edgar White. Both the independent and the aligned commonly write from the perspective of the Black Experience. The Black Arts writers advocate Black Consciousness and Black Revolution, whereas Gordone, Kennedy, and White use the Black Experience as a convenient frame of reference from which to explore the dilemma of the individual in a hostile environment. The promotion of Black Consciousness as a way of life was not seen by these independents as their particular artistic responsibility. In fact, they regarded Black Consciousness as a limiting concept. Having been sensitized and enlightened by their own Black experience, they found parallels between the Black Experience in America and situations involving people of other races and nationalities. But rather than promoting Black Consciousness, they have used their wisdom to enable them to analyze the problems of other oppressed groups, classes, and/or individuals. A sense of universal concern motivated these playwrights.

Edgar White has managed to evade the clutches of genre and ethnic categorizing. His success has been due in large part to a proclivity for disguise. He borrows styles and conventions at will. And just as he is not constrained by any one style or form, neither does he allow himself to be confined to any particular subject matter. White appears to be exceptionally clear and poised in his attitude toward playwriting and toward the human condition, as the following comments reveal:

Critic: You are a young Black playwright in a time of revolution. What are your plays like?

White: My plays are my visions of life. They are not racial polemics but dramas reflecting the human comedy.

Critic: Just what does that mean?

White: It means that I go within myself, get into my own head, and if I'm honest enough, go deep enough, I will speak not only for me but for all men. Life is a comedy because there doesn't seem to be much to it and yet we go on with our "significant" things.[1]

Edgar White was born in the British West Indies and brought to the United States when he was five years old. His individual style is partly a product of his memory of his early life. More importantly, White's interest in architecture is reflected in the remarkably architectonic form of his plays. His ideas are usually original and provocative, but a deft handling of structure is his particular forte.

White based *Burghers of Calais* (1970) on the story of the Scottsboro Boys, intending to represent the Scottsboro Boys as Everyman. In 1931 nine Black youths aged thirteen to twenty, falsely accused of raping two White women, were indicted in Scottsboro, Alabama, and sentenced to die. The incident began on a freight train when a group of White youths antagonized a group of Black youths. When the Black youths forced the White boys off the train, the White boys vowed vengeance. A farmer in whose house the White boys took refuge telephoned ahead of the train to the nearest town of Paint Rock, Alabama. The local sheriff of Paint Rock and a mob of Whites waited to arrest the Black boys. Two White women, dressed in coveralls, were discovered among those on the freight train. Fearing they would be charged with vagrancy and prostitution, the women alleged they had been raped by the nine Black youths. During the first trial in Scottsboro, eight of the youths were sentenced to the electric chair; the ninth, because of his extreme youth, was referred to juvenile court. The case attracted the International Labor Defense (ILD) and the NAACP. The ILD (Communist party) engaged an astute White lawyer from New York to defend the youths. One of the women later retracted her story, but the other woman held to hers. The national and international press chronicled a long series of trials. Finally, in 1937, the state of Alabama, amid rumors of a deal, dropped charges against four of the youths. The remaining five were eventually given long prison sentences. The Scottsboro incident inspired John Wexley's *They Shall Not Die* and Jean-Paul Sartre's *The Reluctant Prostitute*. Wexley's play, produced in 1934, portrays the arrest and trial in the style of social realism. Sartre's "comic" version of the story focuses on the Black man as a scapegoat for immoral, hypocritical White Americans.

The Burghers of Calais, based on *The Scottsboro Boy* (1950) by Earl Conrad and Scottsboro defendant Haywood Patterson, sheds new light on the incident. Patterson's is the only first-hand account of the affair. Patterson was the oldest, largest, and most intrepid of the nine boys. White calls him Bagatelle. The other youths are named Nicknack, Quid, Pro Quo, Three Sad Fellows, and Two Sent to Juvenile Prison.

While the play appears to be modeled after Brecht's epic theatre, it owes its largest debt to Peter Weiss' *Marat/Sade*.[2] Both plays are based on historical events. Both feature a play within a play. *Marat/Sade* is set in an insane asylum, while the drug prison in Lexington, Kentucky, provides the setting for *The Burghers of Calais*. Theatricality is the watchword for both plays.

The Burghers of Calais opens with the Speaker, a Black man wearing shades, addressing an audience composed of prison inmates and invited guests. To amuse the guests at tea time, the inmates put on a play, preceded by a jazz recital. The Speaker announces that the inmates will perform a play written by a prisoner and based on the story of the Scottsboro Boys. Since the prison has among its inmates former lawyers and judges, the actors play themselves.

The Speaker then sets the stage for the performance. The Author also wearing shades, makes his appearance: he smokes a pipe and is dressed stereotypically in corduroy jacket and open-collar white shirt. Four actors representing members of the Communist party (ILD) take seats at a long table inside the Communist Hall and discuss the Scottsboro case. Here one of the play's major themes is established: the Scottsboro Boys were exploited by the small-time politicians in Scottsboro, the power structure in the state of Alabama and the South, as well as by the Communist party and the NAACP. The Leader advises the Communist group: "Oh . . . yes, brothers, we have an opportunity now to get ourselves some much needed publicity."[3]

Act 1, scene 3, occurs at the NAACP headquarters. Two well-dressed, light-skinned Black men and four equally well-dressed dark-skinned Blacks discuss the feasibility of participating in the case. The NAACP seems to have less power than the Communist party and its prominent lawyer. Their indecisiveness and skepticism contrast with the resolute single-mindedness of the Communists. They decide to enter the case as much to block and compete against the party as to serve the cause of human justice.

Scene 4 represents Scottsboro in the unrestrained style of vaudevillian comedy and Molière-type slapstick. The nine boys are in a large cage. Signs that read "I am Negro" or "I am white" hang around the necks of all the characters. The first sub-scene is presided over by the Speaker, who releases the Scottsboro Boys and parades them like circus animals for the audience's inspection. The Speaker separates the two young boys from the others and sends them to juvenile prison. Seven, the Speaker announces, is an ideal number for the burghers of Calais. Suddenly, the seven boys break into a spontaneous Greek dance that lasts about five minutes. The Speaker asks the arresting officer, Sheriff Club Hawk, to describe the arrest. The sheriff presents his account, tries unsuccessfully to force the boys to sign a confession, then announces he is leaving for dinner. He warns the boys to sign a confession upon his return or he will turn them over to the lynch mob, whose voices can be heard off stage.

In the following scene Bagatelle and Nicknack, the two boys taking an active part in the action, talk to one another as if they were two stand-up comics. They sound harmless and quaintly amusing, but subtle bitterness and sarcasm underpin their deceptive naivete:

Speaker: . . . All right. Bagatelle, go on.

Bagatelle: Well, stupid here commence to panic.

Nicknack: I ain't stupid.

Bagatelle: Yes you are, you forget?

Nicknack: Oh yeah, I forgot. I'm stupid.

Bagatelle: Yeah! So, he starts crying and pissing on himself and what not!

Nicknack: Oh Lord, I ain't done nothing wrong, why they going to hang me?

Bagatelle: You were born Black, weren't you? That's what the hell you did wrong.[4]

In the final sub-scene scene, Leiby, the White lawyer, visits the boys in their cells to build up their confidence and morale.

Act 2, comprised of six short scenes, continues to develop the mixed mood of tragedy and farce. The testimony of Miss Ellen Twitromb, the woman holding to her original story, not only reflects the tragedy of the real-life situation but also reveals the absurdity of the belief that all Black males (adults and children) harbor animalistic sexual lust for White women. Leiby attempts to discredit the testimony of Ellen Twitromb by establishing the fact that she is a known prostitute and opportunistic trollop. Susan Docile, the other woman, mysteriously resurfaces out of hiding in scene 5 to tell the court the sad and pathetic story of her deprived life and admits to lying about the rape. The NAACP, now represented by a character neither White nor Black and wearing a question mark about his neck, continues to battle the ILD. Bagatelle and Nicknack, now wiser, take advantage of the situation by appropriating cigarettes, lighters, and other conveniences from the representatives of the ILD, NAACP, and other miscellaneous supporters.

In act 3 the play within breaks down. The actor playing Nicknack complains that he is better than the actor playing the part of Bagatelle and therefore should have that role himself. The Speaker halts the confrontation, insisting that the performance is more important than any other considerations. The Speaker presents Bagatelle's background, and Minister Lazarillo interviews Bella Donna, Bagatelle's mother. Bella Donna is a pious woman but a bitter mother. Bagatelle grows more brave and haughty and he becomes convinced he might "beat the rap." Bagatelle meets the Grand Inquisitor in scene 2 which seems to be dressed in the clothes of Strindberg, straight out of the closet of *A Ghost Sonata*. White uses ambiguous religious symbolism and creates the impression that individuals are linked through an unbroken line of history. The Grand Inquisitor asks a series of banal questions to inquire into Bagatelle's moral character. Bagatelle is questioned about his religious belief, his ancestry, and his relationship with his mother. He lacks any knowledge of an ancestor who was a general from Carthage, nor does he remember whether his mother was pleased or dismayed by his birth. More importantly, Bagatelle does not allow the Grand Inquisitor to trap him into confessing his inveterate immorality and religious corruption. Bagatelle answers fatuous, but incriminating, questions with unexpected adroitness. "How many angels can balance on the end of a pin?" asks the Grand Inquisitor. Bagatelle replies, "Depends on the pin."[5]

The third act explores the aftermath of the Scottsboro incident and leads to the conclusion of the play. The Speaker reports that Three Sad Fellows are paroled after six years, that Nicknack escapes after ten years in prison but returns after having his first sexual adventure with a woman, and that by 1940 world events had thrown the Scottsboro case into obscurity. Scene 5 portrays Bagatelle, Nicknack, Quid, and Pro Quo aboard a "leper ship of fools," which is refused entrance to every port. The seventh and last scene depicts a eucharistic celebration set in the Socialist Meeting Hall. Bagatelle has escaped from prison after serving nineteen years. White frames this final scene in a tabloid of Da Vinci's *Last Supper*. A Bearded Fellow bends over Bagatelle's right shoulder, whispering in his ear. Bagatelle, the honored guest, will be used by the Socialists, just as Christ was used by Judas, to further their selfish goals.

White treats the Scottsboro incident as though it were more myth than fact. Indeed, the true story is a veritable American legend with the power to evoke amazement and concern. The use of epic structure to dramatize the legend identifies Aristotle's *Poetics* as a further source. Comic elements integrated into the play reduce the seriousness of the subject and free the playwright from the obligation to use protest and polemics. The identification of the Scottsboro Boys with Christ, lepers, and the ship of fools demonstrates the universality of man's inhumanity to man. Also, White's objective handling of characters and events—his use of distancing devices, such as the play within a play, and tragicomic elements—creates tension in the audience not by having their sense of reality sharply conflict with the reality on stage but by sobering them, making them more conscious of the comedy, and tragedy, inherent in the human condition.

Fun in Lethe (1970) shows the playwright's virtuosity in handling form and language. More so, perhaps, in this play than in *The Burghers of Calais*, White reveals a remarkable ear for dialects as well as an impressive dexterity with language. The play follows Hamartia (Ham) Tchend, a West Indian poet, through Great Britain. This gives the playwright a chance to capture the dialects of the West Indian, the British upper and lower classes, the Irish scholar, and the English-speaking Pakistani. White uses structural conventions from Chinese classical theatre and Greek comedy. Hamartia writes a complete little verse play titled *Cormorants and Bitterns*, White's parody of Aristophanes. To avoid the typical play-within-a-play format, White has the little play performed in Dublin at Trinity College for special viewing by Mr. Tomas Truegoids, an important person in the Irish theatre. Yet for all its display of structural virtuosity and brilliant language, *Fun in Lethe* simply does not succeed thematically or formally.

The Wonderful Years (1970) looks at life from the point of view of the Puerto Rican. The action is comic improvisational, and according to White, full of *lazzi*, a piece of burlesque in the commedia dell'arte. The play opens with the witch scene from *Macbeth*. This time two old women throw dice and prophesy ruin in Spanish. They announce that the dice reveal this is the day of the death. Life is a toilet, they say. Then, laughing, they creep offstage. White develops the theme of the futility and insanity of life in *The Mummer's Play* (1970) as well as in *The Wonderful Yeare*. Misserimus, the central character in *The Wonderful Yeare*, echoes Bellysong and Pariah from *The Mummer's Play*; Bellysong repeats the comment that life is a toilet. Misserimus is called "the Puerto Rican Picasso." His dubious reputation rests on a single painting called *Madonna in Chains*, from which the chains are excluded. Misserimus is vain and romantic, and this, he explains to his mother, Mamacita, is not easy to do in hell. His exquisite gift of gab and his irresistible personal appeal draw the lovely Maria to him, but his marriage is a romantic gesture and an economic necessity. Maria has made up her mind to escape the fate of most Puerto Rican women. She wants to get far away from the ugly deprivation that surrounds her and shed her Puerto Rican identity. Yet her attraction to Misserimus' charm, a mixture of fatalism and romantic vanity, binds her to the fate she wants to avoid. They marry, and Misserimus immediately puts Maria to work to support him while he paints masterpieces that, he says, are twenty years ahead of the critics.

The play's title is a cruel pun. Just as the women prophesied, this is the day—or year—of the death, for a plague has struck the city of New York. The playwright asks the play be seen in a universal perspective. The audience must interpret the plague as they see it. Decay and devastation infest Spanish Harlem. A rat runs across the floor of Misserimus' parents' apartment; Mamacita's frightened screams interrupt a heated argument between Don Hernando (Misserimus' brother-in-law) and the rat, which symbolizes the plague, and seems to be an allusion to Albert Camus' *The Plague*. In this play the plague smybolizes the physical and moral deterioration of New York City, a condition which exacerbates the squalid living conditions in Spanish Harlem. Amid poverty, crime, and political oppression, Misserimus' friends express rage and disillusionment with the conditions of their lives and the lives of their fellow Puerto Ricans. Milton is a revolutionary. The sensitive and profound Raul aspires to be a lawyer so he can serve the Puerto Rican people through law. Raul goes insane from thinking too much about the absurdity of life. Also a painter, as well as nonpolitical and realistic, Tomasio is a foil to his three friends. Although he acknowledges the economic and cultural deprivation of his people, he senses futility in the attempt by his friends to change conditions. He accepts life as it is and symbolizes those people who accommodate themselves to "the plague." Raul and Milton, however, are more committed to changing society for the benefit of Puerto Ricans. They are the play's existential heroes; in Raul's mental breakdown is projected the nihilism of those individuals who are convinced all efforts to derive meaning in life are futile.

As Mamacita dies—her death blamed on the "vapors" from the plague—Misserimus begins to change. At the funeral Tomasio remarks to Misserimus that a change has occurred in his painting style—he is now painting still lifes and portraits. After Mamacita's death he becomes even more conventional, assuming a teaching position at the New School. Despite Misserimus' finding a purpose for his life, the plague continues to spread death and destruction. Ironically, the play ends on a note of hope, leading Richard Harrier to proclaim the "play is about the gift of life in the midst of death."[6]

The Crucificado (1972) continues the investigation into the inscrutable inanities of humankind. This time the burden of vision is borne by Morose, an architect and writer. Morose, a mulatto of a Trinidadian and Spanish descent, searches for peace. He finds, instead, that there is no sense to the world or meaning in human endeavor. He commits mental and spiritual suicide, enslaving himself to heroin and sex. His only salvation from the bleak and hopeless world around him and from complete insanity or death has been his two lovers, Soledada (light-skinned and dependable) and Celestina (dark-skinned and moody). Three beggars represent his consciousness, the various personas of his id. Gongora is an old blind poet, the embodiment of two legends, one Greek, the other Hebrew. He is a Tiresian figure in that he has been both male and female, and he symbolizes the Biblical figure of Ham in that he was pun-

ished (blinded) for looking upon his father while he was na-
ked. Pedro is a mirror image of his oppressors, and Rafael is
fiery and sensitive.

A chance of a lifetime comes Morose's way in the person of
El Cid, the father who deserted him and his mother in Trini-
dad. Now a wealthy man whose only devoted companion is his
mulatto niece, El Cid represents all the greed, exploitation, and
corruption rampant in the world. He began as a small-time
manufacturer of toilet paper, but he has expanded his business
to include other enterprises, some legal and others not so legal.
He wants to make amends with his son, Morose, first by send-
ing him on a world tour and then by giving him a partnership
in the business. In her soliloquy El Cid's niece concludes her
uncle's guilt is the cause of his generosity to Morose. El Cid
has made a fortune off dope only to discover his son is a junky.

The trip around the world makes Morose more morose. When
he and Soledada, who had accompanied him, return to the
States, he reports few positive impressions. Of course, El Cid
is eager to find out whether the trip has changed Morose in any
way. His questions are typical and mundane:

El Cid: . . . You've had a chance to see how other people live. Have
you learned anything?
Morose: Yes, people are asleep or hungry.[7]

Finally, Morose can achieve the inner peace he seeks in one way
only. He kills El Cid, symbolically freeing himself, an effect il-
lustrated when old Gongora gets a momentary glimpse of light.

The plays of Adrienne Kennedy reflect a preoccupation with
the workings of the collective unconscious and with the emotions of fear and guilt. She is fascinated with archetypal symbolism and uses bizarre psychological imagery to explore the
consciousness of a peculiarly contemporary individual. James
Hatch and Ted Shine characterize her style as one concerned
with "the paradoxes of Spirit and Flesh; Black and White; Past
and Present."[8] These paradoxes are usually explored within a
single mind. This single consciousness reveals the mental and
spiritual alienation most individuals suffer. She is mostly concerned with what Sartre has called lived experiences, a term

coined as an alternative for the overworked *consciousness*. In Adrienne Kennedy's plays these lived experiences are usually of three types: those actually lived, those imagined, and those that might be called eidetic. All three types are portrayed in *Funnyhouse of a Negro* (1964), the central figure of which is a young woman named Sarah.

Kennedy's play rests on the premise that contemporary man—especially Euro- and Afro-Americans—has broken with his collective unconscious. He is psychologically and spiritually alienated from fellow beings past and present, and adrift in his own mind. *Funnyhouse of a Negro* deals with the problem of sorting out one's identity. Besides Sarah, the characters in the play are the Mother, the Landlady (Funnylady), and Raymond (Funnyman). Sarah's various identities are represented as the Duchess of Hapsburg, Queen Victoria, Patrice Lumumba, and Jesus. The Funnyhouse with its many rooms—the Hapsburg chamber, the chamber in a Victoria Castle, the hotel where she thinks she kills her father, and the jungle—are places inside Sarah's mind, where she and all her identities live. Raymond and the Landlady are the only characters who are not "selves" of Sarah, although they too are projections of her mind. They function as a chorus linking the world of the mind on the stage with the more concrete world inhabited by the audience. The play utilizes highly poetic, cryptic, and sardonic dialogue. Variations on a single theme, also characteristic of the play's language, call to mind qualities of improvisational jazz.

Kennedy's vivid description of Sarah and her lifestyle demonstrates playwriting skill of a high order. Sarah most often speaks through her alter egos, but Kennedy also portrays her social life. Sarah has just graduated from a city college where she majored in English. She occasionally works in libraries, but she spends the majority of her time writing poetry in the style of Edith Sitwell. She lives in a small room in a brownstone on the Upper West Side of New York City. Her room is filled with old books, and photographs of castles and the monarchs of England. She also dreams a great deal, and when she talks the dream world mixes with the real world. Her father was a dark-skinned Black man ("the blackest of them all"), and her mother was an extremely fair-skinned Black woman. Sarah has "pale-yellow skin" and "no glaring Negroid features," but she does lament the fact that her hair is "frizzy" and "kinky." She dates a Jewish boy (Raymond) who also writes poetry and has an interest in Black people. On the surface Sarah appears to be ordinary, but these surface events are just only a minuscule part of her life. Sarah's lived experiences also include significant eidetic events—vicarious experiences as well as stories told her by her mother and father. Since she is a part of her parents, their fears, disillusionments, and feelings of guilt are passed on to her, absorbed osmotically into her subconscious. Moreover, Sarah's condition is highly symbolic; the fear and guilt she experiences are representative of the fear and guilt of all Black people, and of all humanity.

The play's structure is somewhat unorthodox. Ostensibly a one-act play, it is divided into two parts. The first part, comprising roughly one-third of the play, serves as a kind of prologue. It ends with the line "He is very interested in Negroes." The stage directions which follow form a bridge between the last line of the prologue and the remaining part of the play, which begins with the line "The characters are myself: the Duchess of Hapsburg, Queen Victoria Regina, Jesus, Patrice Lumumba."[9] Symbols and images that in the prologue are personal to Sarah's subconscious become, in the latter part of the play, universalized to exemplify contemporary man's collective unconscious. For example, the scene in Africa, close to the end of the play, depicts the dialectical conflict between the biblical and the scientific theories of the origin of the species. Jesus, one of Sarah's identities, explains: "I am going to Africa and kill this Black man named Patrice Lumumba. Why? Because all my life I believed my Holy Father to be God, but now I know that my father is a Black man."[10] The Bible cites Genesis as the beginning of mankind and established God as the Creator and the Father of Jesus. Conversely, anthropologist Richard Leakey uses the scientific approach to hypothesize that mankind originated in Africa.[11] This theory suggests that man's early ancestors derived from a geographical area inhabited and historically identified with the Negroid race. Enough credibility has been given this theory to arouse alarm and dismay among the most devout. Jesus, then, early in the play becomes generally symbolic of the human race, and, with obvious sarcasm intended, especially representative of the Caucasian race. Somewhat agitated, Jesus speaks both for the Hebrews and all Caucasian people when he declares: "Through my apocalypses and my raging sermons I have tried to escape him, through God Almighty I have tried to escape being Black." Certainly, Jesus speaks for militant exponents of White supremacy who have appropriated and perverted Christian doctrine in an effort to justify their exploitative and nihilistic behaviors, but He speaks also for Sarah and her mother, who both wanted to escape their Blackness. Patrice Lumumba is a symbol in this dialectic of Africa—the father of humankind and the progenitor of Jesus. Jesus' rage is the rage of all White, derivative races.

The facts that we learn about Sarah's missionary father provide added depth to her characterization as "the Negro." Landlady reports that Sarah's father had begged her forgiveness for having left Africa, for after his departure, Lumumba was murdered. The father's resultant guilt feelings at having abandoned Lumumba to his death are symbolized by the loss of hair (a motif that saturates the play) that afflicts Sarah's mother and implicates the Black race. The loss of hair associates both the race and the individual with extreme feelings of guilt and fear. Sarah's mother lost her hair because she felt fear and guilt at believing her near-White body and heritage had been defiled by Sarah's father's Black touch. Black Americans lost their hair because they abandoned Lumumba and his revolutionary struggle, because they rejected their Blackness, and because they disavowed any collective responsibility for the plight of Black Africans with whom they have a propinquity. (The extent of this collective guilt is also expressed by Aime Cesaire in his play *A Season in the Congo*. The devious Mokutu (Mobutu), to ingratiate himself with the Congolese people, delivers a stirring speech in the wake of Lumumba's assassination in which he proclaims, "The piety of a nation will never cease to make reparation for our crime, the crime of which we are all guilty.")[12]

Funnyhouse of a Negro is a lyrical comment on the conditions of modern man: guilt, fear, and disintegration. All of us feel this searing guilt because of our gross insensitivity and inhumanity to each other. All of us are numbed by fear of discovering the truth of our own being and the real source of our existence. The fear of discovery and the guilt stemming from abandoning our own kind distort our sense of identity and become the source of our psychological and cultural disintegration. Our desperate denial of the universal unconscious and the obsessive refutation of the fact of our common ancestry—the interrelatedness of all races—are reflected in Sarah's chaotic psychological condition.

Luckily, the pieces are all pulled together in the final passages of the play, which alternate swiftly between the African bush, Sarah's father's apartment, and Sarah's own room. At this point all the disparate identities suddenly merge in the person of Jesus. The integration of the fragmented selves into one composite mind permits Sarah to perceive herself both universally and individually. She is herself, Sarah, as well as the embodiment of the human life continuum. The truth of mankind, then, whether we want to admit it or not, is expressed in Jesus' words: "They told me my father was God but my father is Black. . . . I am tied to a Black Negro."[13] But the weight of the truth and the burden of knowledge is too much for Sarah/Jesus. She tries first to exorcise from her consciousness the demon of her affliction, her father—the accursed Negro—by bludgeoning him with an "ebony head." But it is Sarah who finally dies by hanging herself. Raymond (Funnyman) attempts to obscure the facts in the play: he reverses the story Sarah tells of herself and her father and discredits her claim that her father hanged himself in grief over Lumumba's murder. "Her father is a doctor, married to a white whore," Raymond alleges, adding: "He is a nigger who eats his meals on a white glass table."[14] Sarah's father is described as the type of Black man who despises his Blackness and aspires to be White, the stereotypical image of Blacks most Whites prefer. By accusing Sarah of being a "funny little liar," Raymond refutes her personal story as well as her reinterpretation of mankind's history and perverts both into a callous myth more palatable to an audience of typical Whites and Blacks.

Kennedy's *A Rat's Mass* (1967) is a surrealistic allegory. This grotesque spectacle cartoons the evils of oppression and fascism, and the religious themes so heavily stressed in *Funny-*

house of a Negro again receive lavish treatment. The characters in the play are Rosemary, Brother Rat, Sister Rat, Mary, Joseph, Two Wise Men, and a Shepherd. Brother and Sister Rat are part human and part rat. Brother Rat, for example, has a rat's head atop a human body; he also has a rat's tail. Although Sister Rat has a human head, she has a rat's belly and a tail. Rosemary (a Medusa figure) has worms in her hair.

In *A Rat's Mass* Kennedy returns to the themes of guilt, fear, and disintegration. She also repeats the technique of merging personalities, themes, and events. Again, the world on stage is depicted as the subjective world of the mind. Real, rational events from history give way to imagined historical events. Again, Kennedy depicts three types of consciousness: the Jewish consciousness of the Nazi Holocaust, the Black Consciousness of the Civil Rights struggle, and the individual states of consciousness of Brother Rat, Sister Rat, and Rosemary. The presence of Jesus, Joseph, Mary, Two Wise Men, and a Shepherd makes historical time irrelevant. The action resolves into a statement: a major characteristic of the majority of human beings, past and present, is a tendency to evade the fact of their cowardice through guilt feelings and irrational religious resignation.

Brother and Sister Rat, also named Blake and Kay, are being hunted down by Nazi soldiers and have been forced to hide in a rat-infested chapel. They partake of Communion in their last Mass before their anticipated execution. Rosemary, a devout Catholic and proud descendant of "the Pope" and Julius Caesar, had persuaded Brother and Sister Rat to embrace Catholicism. Brother Rat, Sister Rat, and Rosemary grew up together in the American Midwest. Blake and Kay adored Rosemary. She was the prettiest girl in their school. They worshipped her also because of her glorious Italian ancestry and felt obscure in comparison. Blake fell in love with Rosemary and wanted to marry her.

The Rat's Chapel is an imaginary setting, a reflection of the psychological condition of the three principal characters. Kay has suffered a severe mental breakdown and projects the dominant themes and abnormalities. At the core of her psychosis is a harrowing memory. Years before, on a slide in the playground in the Midwestern town, she was brutally raped by a gang of boys which her imagination has now transformed into a squad of Nazi soldiers. The image of Rosemary with worms in her hair had appeared at the top of the slide. Kay now imagines herself to be pregnant and her brother Blake to be the father of their "rat baby." Moreover, Brother Rat begs Rosemary for salvation, and she advises him to commit suicide. Images of Rosemary as holy and beautiful conflict with images of her as vile and malevolent. She embodies the collusion of Catholicism and Fascism in a period of universal degeneracy. Rosemary has opted for conformity with the Fascists, while the other oppressed people(s) have resigned themselves to being frightened rats, trying desperately to hide themselves in attics to escape detection by the infamous gray cats (Nazi soldiers) that walk the houses (streets). The play ends with the arrival of a procession of shotgun-toting Nazi soldiers. Blake and Kay fall after being fired upon, but Rosemary remains standing.

Adrienne Kennedy's somewhat oblique contribution to the Black Theatre Movement comes in the form of a work entitled *Sun: A Poem for Malcolm X Inspired by His Death*. First performed at La Mama Experimental Theatre Club (Cafe La Mama), with an improvisational "Free Jazz" accompaniment by the Ornette Coleman Double Quartet, the piece requires only one actor. Much in the manner of Baraka's *Ba-Ra-Ka*, *Sun* combines poetry and body movement to create dramatic intensity through the coordination of auditory and kinesthetic imagery. It abandons decorative scenery and utilizes brightly colored lights and costumes. It calls for sound effects (usually, but not always, music), improvisational play with lights, and the occasional use of rear-screen projections. The play abandons characters and dialogue and attempts less to tell a story than to illustrate a particular theme through verbal and visual images. In most cases the entire piece is just movement built around, or into, a single poem. This form of "choreopoetry" eventually found fuller expression in Ntozake Shange's highly successful *For Colored Girls Who Have Considered Suicide When the Rainbow is Enuf*.

Though Gordone, White, and Kennedy prefer to sing to their own muse, one cannot deny that they have made a valuable contribution to the theatre generally and to the modest but influential and still-expanding oeuvre of the Black Theatre Movement in particular. These playwrights seem to believe that human experience is unitary, but they also demonstrate that Black Consciousness is a progressive force challenging the stagnation and inertia of human nature and human institutions. Their particular Black Consciousness is conditioned by keen sensibility as well as by strong political commitment. Surely, the harmonious co-existence of personal sensibility and social and political commitment is a precondition of any effective revolutionary action. The Non-Polemical Structuralist playwrights, then, may not be overtly preoccupied with immediate and topical aspects of race relations in the United States, but they have demonstrated that they are seriously concerned with the politics of freedom and identity as they affect all individuals oppressed by governments, outmoded customs, and rampant ignorance.

NOTES

1. Edgar White, *Underground: Four Plays by Edgar White* (New York: William Morrow and Co., 1970), dustcover.

2. Richard Harrier, Foreword to *Underground: Four Plays by Edgar White*, by Edgar White (New York: William Morrow and Co., 1970), p. vi.

3. White, *Underground*, p. 9.

4. White, *Underground*, p. 16.

5. White, *Underground*, p. 42.

6. Harrier, "Foreword," p. vi.

7. Edgar White, *The Crucificado: Two Plays by Edgar White* (New York: William Morrow and Co., 1973), p. 142.

8. James V. Hatch and Ted Shine, eds., *Black Theatre USA: 45 Plays by Black Americans, 1847–1974* (New York: The Free Press, 1974), p. 756.

9. Adrienne Kennedy, "Funnyhouse of a Negro," in *Anthology of the American Negro in the Theatre*, ed. Lindsay Patterson (New York: Publishers Co., 1967), p. 283.

10. Kennedy, "Funnyhouse of a Negro," p. 289.

11. Richard Leakey and Roger Lewin, "Origins of the Mind," *Psychology Today* 12 (July 1978): 51.

12. Aime Cesaire, *A Season in the Congo* (New York: Grove Press/Evergreen Edition, 1969), p. 103.

13. Kennedy, "Funnyhouse," p. 289.

14. Kennedy, "Funnyhouse," p. 290.

Conclusion

On the surface, the Black Theatre Movement of the 1960s and 1970s might easily appear to have been unsuccessful. Overall, it certainly cannot be said that the movement effected any dynamic change within the American theatre per se. In fact, in many ways it seems the movement was a creature of its times and was fated, like most vulnerable species, either to expire with the evolution of a new era or to live on tenaciously as a relic of the past. But it is curious that of the many theatre movements alive during the epoch, the Black Theatre Movement is one of the few—if not the only one—still surviving. The evolutionary process has shown that species soon become extinct when they cease to adapt to change or when they are swallowed up into the evolutionary vortex. The Black Theatre Movement in the United States, which was born as long ago as 1821–22, has proven to be a remarkable adapter to any new environmental challenges, and since those who were and are participants in the movement have still not been completely absorbed into the cultural/theatrical mainstream, the movement's existence is assured for some time to come.

However, the future viability of the Black Theatre Movement also depends upon its having a permanent audience. The movement has always needed sustained interest in Black Theatre as a legitimate and vital outlet continually serving the daily spiritual, psychological, and cultural needs of the people. But the various and recurring attempts for over a century and a half to build a monolithic Black Theatre have turned out to be little more than moments of passing interest or transitory fads. The

Black Theatre Movement of the 1960s and 1970s, then, as all other past forms of Black Theatre, can be described as a theatre movement in search of an audience. It should be made clear that ever since the 1920s, when Eugene O'Neill and others experimented with Black subject matter, there has always been some interest in, if not a demand for, plays with Black-oriented themes. But these plays, in order to be financially successful, must serve the special needs of an audience interested neither in supporting a permanent Black Theatre nor in being truly informed. Obviously, then, the Black musical has been far more successful than the "serious" Black plays on and off Broadway.

In the beginning, when *The Blacks* made its 1961 American debut, and when *Dutchman* came later in 1963–64, there was a receptive audience. An important point to keep in mind, however, is that the particular audience attending these plays was the same audience that might have also attended a Living Theatre fare or the Off-Broadway production of Tennessee Williams' *Camino Real*. In other words, this was an audience of young professionals and older, more seasoned theatre buffs seeking a retreat from the dullness of Broadway. This was, then, a special type of audience, the same audience that had read Kafka, had read or at least heard of Antonin Artaud, and attended foreign films. On the other hand, this was an audience conditioned by education and a middle-class background. It was an audience of liberals or pseudosophisticates who thought it fashionable to appear to be liberal-minded.

The point is, the audience that paid first attention to the plays presenting the "new Black mood" was invariably the same audience interested in avant-garde theatre. It might sound strange, but the precursors of the 1960s Black Theatre Movement, plays such as *The Blacks*, *Dutchman*, and *The Baptism* (a 1964 satire by Baraka), were plays bearing the imprint of absurdist drama. For certainly it was from the French-based avant-garde—set in motion by the works of Sartre and Camus during the early post–World War II years—that a fecundity of theatre movements starting in the 1950s and spreading through the early 1970s originated. Although a myriad of theatre groups arose, with as many different philosophies and purposes, they all had in common with the absurdist plays the objective of wreaking havoc in the theatre and thus destroying false conceptions about reality and the theatrical experience. Soon it became expected for this type of "revolutionary" or "radical" theatre to be, if not truly shocking, then pleasantly disturbing and revolting.

When the Black Theatre Movement broke away from the avant-garde fold, when it sought an identity and purpose more commensurate with the social and political goals of the Black group, it lost its original source of audience support. For one thing, by espousing a social commitment, the Black Theatre artists could no longer afford to be as theatrically and thematically daring as the more experimental groups. So when the Black Theatre assumed a commitment to social relevancy, it was necessary for it to retain, not cast off, the illusion of coherence. The more adventuresome theatre movements of the times opted for a theatre built around ambiguity and mystery. Still, the central priority of the radical theatre groups was the same as that of the Black Theatre—to break down the artificial barrier between audience and actors and to blend the real world with the imitated world on stage. But the so-called radical theatre addressed itself to the needs of an audience with an essentially Euro-American consciousness, while the Black Theatre fashioned techniques designed to lift the consciousness of Blacks by purging them of the alleged corrupting influences of debilitating Euro-American consciousness. The Black Theatre Movement, therefore, by directing its message away from the dominant White audience, created a vacuum with the anticipation that it would be filled by an eager Black audience. The Black Theatre, then, set a double task for itself, seeking not only to develop a unique form of theatre but also to develop the audience needed to receive and appreciate this particular form.

Interestingly, the radical forms of Black Theatre, those based on the Black Arts tenets of Black Aestheticism, always stayed closely allied with the "New Black Poetry" movement. In other words, Black Theatre groups were most likely to spring up around Black poetry workshops, where other forms of the Black Aesthetic, such as dance and music, were also being pursued. This was especially true of theatre groups such as the original Black Arts Repertory Theatre of Harlem, the Free Southern Theater (during and after the tenure of Tom Dent), and Spirit

House. For one thing, these performing poetry troupes could reach Black audiences outside the Manhattan-Broadway vicinity and could stage their readings in makeshift conditions— storefronts, church basements, high school and college auditoriums, and even outdoors.

The audience that took interest in the New Black Poetry, and eventually in the New Black Drama, was primarily a young, predominantly college-based audience. Productions of works by Baraka, Bullins, Caldwell, Sanchez, and Milner were often restaged by Black Theatre groups on large, predominantly white campuses. It was usually the most radical of the Black Theatre plays that appealed especially to this young college audience. Clearly, this audience was better educated, more middle-class-oriented, and more ideological than the "grass-roots" Blacks that the Black Theatre playwrights were more eager to reach. Granted, many of these radicalized college students came from grass-roots environments; but the degree to which they epitomized "the people" is somewhat minimal. With the possible exception of El Teatro Campesino, which actively involved itself in protest demonstrations resulting in clashes with the police, the Black Theatre, like the other radical theatre movements of the 1960s, found support principally among the intellectual left and young cultural/political rebels. Consequently, when the powerful counterrevolutionary machine instituted by the first Nixon administration declared war against "insurgency" within the United States, a reactionary backlash occurred. One significant effect was that the strong ideological rhetoric associated with radical theatre groups caused them once again to become alienated from their audience.

Viewed from yet another perspective, the Black Theatre Movement of the 1960s and 1970s, contrary to popular belief, was more bilateral than unilateral. The movement was, in other words, split into two distinct camps. One side was composed of writers advocating a Black Aesthetic, Black Consciousness, and sociopolitical revolt. The other side was represented by professional theatre artists who viewed Black Theatre as their only means of acquiring work, training, experience, and a receptive audience for plays dealing primarily with the Black Experience. From this comparison, it can be seen that the Black

Theatre Movement has within itself both an avant-garde theatre and a more traditional theatre, and the two factions were at
odds when it came to ideology and the approach used to change
conditions for Blacks both within the American system per se
and within the American theatre. It is certainly curious (and almost ironic) that the divided factions of the Black Theatre
Movement each espoused, though in different ways, the philosophy of Black Nationalism and Black Separatism. But again,
the significant factor is that while one group advocated the highly
racial Black Nationalist politics of men such as Elijah Muham-
mad and Malcolm X, the other group opted for a more mod-
erate form of Black Nationalism based on a willingness to compromise in face of entrenched racist attitudes existing within the
American theatre framework. One group, therefore, viewed
Blackness as a viable ideology. But the other group saw Blackness as a fateful situation that needed to be dealt with in an
objective manner. The best example of the latter attitude can be
read into a statement by Douglas Turner Ward regarding the
continued use of the term *Negro* by the Negro Ensemble Company:

At the time we got started, the word "black" was just in its ascen-
dancy and "Negro" was being given an almost pejorative connotation.
I felt that was wrong. The word "Negro" has a long, honored history.
I like "black"—it makes a positive statement about what we are—but
I loathed the posturing and attitudinizing that went with the total put-
down of the word "Negro."[1]

The "eclectics" tended also to blur clear-cut lines of polari-
zation within the Black Theatre Movement. These were the
playwrights who found it convenient to switch postures from
time to time rather than stick to one particular style. In most
cases what distinguished the Black Consciousness playwrights
from the less ideological ones was simply the rhetoric ex-
pounded. By far the most successful eclectic was Ed Bullins. One
minute Bullins can be found experimenting with absurdist forms
in such works as *How Do You Do?* and *The Electronic Nigger*. The
next minute the playwright is discovered wading in a naturalistic stream with plays such as *In the Wine Time* and *Goin' a Buf-*

falo. Nonetheless, besides Baraka, Bullins was at the forefront of the revolutionary theatre. Indeed, Bullins best exemplifies the tendency by some Blacks Arts writers to use rhetoric, rather than practice, to divide themselves from the less ideological Black playwrights as well as from the other forms of theatre.

Is this to say, then, that the more radical forms of the Black Theatre Movement were couched more in theory than in the worked-out mechanics of a special dramaturgy? To be sure, the ideas and concepts outlined by Baraka and Bullins for their, respectively, "Revolutionary Theatre" and "Theatre of Reality" were innovative and provocative. But the guiding force behind the desire to develop a distinct Black Theatre in the first place was the Civil Rights Movement taking place in America. Therefore, the ritualistic rhetoric of Black Power and ordinary theatre jargon often mixed and sometimes clashed. And, once the idea of a unique Black Aesthetic was added to these other two elements, the blueprint for a clearly defined Black Theatre was sometimes lost in a welter of language. Thus the result was usually more in keeping with the visionary ideas of Artaud, rather than the more lucid, objective formula for Brecht's Epic Theatre.

Conversely, the artists of the traditional theatre group displayed no such conflict between dicta and practical goals. Simply, their objective was to build a dependable audience and to ensure, first, that actors and technicians received training and experience, and second, that these theatre artists found sufficient work as professionals. Such is not to imply, however, that this practical-minded group was accommodationist or counterrevolutionary. Their main objection (as voiced by Douglas Turner Ward) to the Black Arts-backed theatre faction, and especially to the Black Revolutionary Theatre, was that it had failed to attract a sizable supportive audience because of second-rate plays. In fact, playwright and drama professor Owen Dodson was even more uncompromising in his criticism of certain trends predominant in the Black Theatre Movement during the 1960s. Dodson writes: "So many of our black playwrights are so saturated with the idea of black oppression, which of course they should be, that they have left out the lasting power, the universality, of their art."[2]

Still, the reality looms large that the Black Theatre Movement, in all its forms during the 1960s and 1970s, was motivated by a sense of exigency. The needs that it sought to remedy were felt to be crucial and urgent. Minds had to be prepared for the coming revolution, and training, experience, and work were desperately needed to offset a century of disadvantage. Yet, in all fairness, it must be realized that all involved with the thrust for a Black Theatre Movement during this period were seriously concerned with presenting a universal view of the human condition, as well as providing genuine artistic expression. That they were universal in focusing so intently on human oppression is supported somewhat by Sartre's observation that the majority of the world's population is struggling under some type of oppression. Their works draw upon the Black spiritual and cultural ethos for their uniqueness and lasting value. Obviously, any attempt to evaluate the Black Theatre Movement without taking into consideration its avowed intentions and purposes is both unfair and reflects an attitude of critical provincialism.

Development, or refinement, of a Black Aesthetic was uppermost to the founders and supporters of the Black Arts Movement. Broadly speaking, the Black Aesthetic was to become the foundation of all relevant Black literature, poetry, music, theatre, and criticism. Invariably, the infrastructure for the Black Aesthetic was found in Black music, but its superstructure was comprised of a mixture of sociological, political, and cultural dialectics. Still, again, the creation of a viable Black Aesthetic, although ambitiously conceived, represented, more or less, yet another alternative to an entrenched and seemingly intractable Europeanized iconography. Consequently, in light of the overall impact the Black Aesthetic has on Black people and the society as a whole, it now appears that the movement had all along given the impression of being merely iconoclastic rather than devastatingly revolutionary. For, obviously, the Black Aesthetic—or racial ethos—had already pervaded every aspect of American life from modern and popular music to athletics and language. Nonetheless, the idea of a Black Aesthetic was germane in guiding and shaping some of the most stimulating and original poetry and theatre productions during the period.

Therefore, for a better understanding of the motives, principles, and values espoused by the exponents of the Black Arts Movement, including those in the theatre, it is necessary to offer an outline for such an aesthetic. The best synopsis of the elements and characteristics that a Black Aesthetic might include is given by Theodore Hudson in his book on Baraka.

Within the purview of the theatre, responsibility for implementing such a blueprint would seem to fall more onto the shoulders of the playwright. It was, incidentally, from a 1937 essay written by Richard Wright, "Blue-print for a Negro Literature," that the basic ideas for a viable and socially valuable Black literature came. But, for this format to be applied to the theatre, directors and actors would also have to work toward its full implementation. Therefore, those playwrights who were perceived as most rebellious—Baraka, Marvin X, Sanchez, and sometimes Bullins—eventually found it necessary to establish their own companies or form alliances with companies that shared their philosophy. When a union of this type was formed, there was likely to be a striving toward the realization of all elements of the Black Aesthetic, while on the other hand, the more traditional and practical companies such as the Negro Ensemble Company produced works by playwrights who were still influenced by more or less conventional forms. Still other companies, the New Lafayette for example, were somewhat middle-of-the-road, remaining flexible enough to oscillate between standard realism such as Milner's *Who's Got His Own* and experimental plays such as Richard Wesley's formidable *Black Terror*. Nonetheless, the mood and temperament of the times made it necessary for practically all Black playwrights and predominantly Black theatre companies to espouse at least a few of the concepts within the Black Aesthetic. For instance, the Negro Ensemble Company, while probably rejecting almost everything else, would accept item 2 under "Style" as well as item 1 under "Philosophy" (see table 1). However, the playwrights were not the only people in the theatre committed to developing a unique form of theatre based on the blueprint for a Black Aesthetic. Barbara Ann Teer, primarily an actress and director, has had tremendous success with her National Black Theatre. The National Black Theatre, in fact, has gone the way

Table 1
ELEMENTS IN THE BLACK AESTHETIC.

Style	Form	Content	Philosophy
1. Rejection of outmoded Western literary styles, as well as repudiation of a provincial Western concept of universality.	1. Experimentation to discover new, unique forms and techniques peculiar to the Black Experience.	1. Content strongly ethnocentric, and based on the concept of Black Nationalism.	1. Identification with the Black masses.
2. Utilization of Black cultural elements (lifestyle and value system), urban and rural Black folk elements, Black language and energetic diction.			2. Rejection of Euro-American cultural values, and their replacement with a Black value system.
			3. (Re)cultivation of the traditional African (collective-communal) concept of "We" as opposed to the individual-istic (more Western) "I."
			4. Belief that art should be functional (not art for art's sake), especially in achieving social, political, and economic goals.

Table compiled from Theodore R. Hudson's *From LeRoi Jones to Amiri Baraka*.[3]

of theatre groups such as the Living Theatre, the Open Theatre, and the Performance Group in rejecting the literary prescript for a presentational format that is non-scripted and collective.

If Charles Gordone is to be taken seriously as a theatre critic and authority, then there was never any such phenomenon as a Black Theatre or a Black Theatre Movement. For while Gordone does concede that there were and are Black playwrights, he contradicts any claim of a bona fide Black Theatre. Thus, according to Gordone, the Black Theatre, especially during the 1960s and early 1970s, was, if anything, an invisible institution. In other words, Gordone makes it seem that the notion of a Black Theatre Movement was merely romantic and self-serving political sermonizing. Gordone's view is important in that it illuminates two major points. For one thing, the differences in philosophy and purpose between the artists of the theatre group and the Black Arts group are emphatically demonstrated through statements made by a member of the former group (Gordone). On the other hand, the attitude reveals the danger in attempting to isolate the Black Theatre Movement from the larger Black Power and Civil Rights Movements of the period. Leland M. Griffin points out that movements get started whenever some pivotal person or group, growing intolerant of imposed exclusion from the society, decides that they have had enough. This grievance then becomes the source of a "felt need," unifying the disgruntled factions into a cohesive force. The unity of the collective is achieved through a mutual understanding of what is causing the discontent and how the cause can be eliminated. Griffin gives a clear explanation of the means by which this mutual understanding is manifested to the dissenters:

It may be called a constitution, manifesto, covenant, program, proclamation, declaration, tract for the times, statement, or counterstatement. It may be expressed in the form of an essay, document, speech, poem, sermon, novel, play, pamphlet or song. Whatever its label or mode of expression, it constitutes the initial act of the movement—the axe raised to its full height, and permitted to fall; or less militantly, the verbal bud from which the movement will unfold into flower.[4]

Certainly, a movement can be militant or nonviolent or both. The main thing is that all factions are galvanized by the feeling of alienation and hostility from the other members/groups within their society. Both factions within the Black Theatre, therefore, had ample reason to effect a movement, together or separately. One would be hard put to deny that something of this nature did not actually happen during the 1960s and 1970s.

But, also, the exoneration of Black people from a negative public image as well as from a debilitating self-image was of central importance to all parties committed to the development of relevant Black Theatre. Although expectations of certain achievable results were always the same, the means by which different playwrights, directors, or theatre groups went about accomplishing these goals sometimes differed. For instance, in terms of rhetorical style, three reasonably clear-cut approaches were evident—the persuasive, the informative, and the inspirational. The moralistic and reverse-psychology approach used by Baraka was persuasive in that it attempted to arouse the Black audience to action. Baraka emphasized the need for Blacks to build self-confidence, to be more self-assertive, and to become aggressive in meeting violence with violence. Moreover, what Bullins has termed Black dialectics—the dialectics of change and the dialectics of experience—needs elucidation. Thus, through the medium of drama, Bullins and those playwrights he speaks of sought to inform their audiences of vital issues concerning "black survival and future . . . and the dreadful white reality of being a modern black captive and victim."[5] Though while Bullins was mainly concerned with stressing the need for self-knowledge, those playwrights who seemed to write realistic evocations of Black family life were providing inspiration for their audiences in another way. Consequently, plays such as *Ceremonies in Dark Old Men*, *The Sty of the Blind Pig*, and *The River Niger* by depicting the Black family in crisis, unveiled unknown (and unsuspected) levels of human courage, sacrifice, and mental fortitude. Although Black playwrights used different approaches to playwriting, they all were instrumental in improving the image of Black people within the contemporary American theatre. Their contribution helps support Sidney

Finkelstien's observation in *Existentialism and Alienation in American Literature*:

One of the achievements of contemporary American Negro literature, aside from its artistic values, is its service in liberating the Negro people from the public image in which they have been cast not only by racists but well-meaning friends who shape the image to fit their own drives and frustrations.[6]

Now that we are in the decade of the 1980s, some people are asking, Has Black Theatre moved beyond revolution? As worded, such a question certainly suggests that the Black Theatre Movement of the 1960s and 1970s, in spite of diversity, will be remembered for its activist and Black Nationalist image. Of course, this should prove that the Black Theatre in the United States does indeed have an image of its own. Also, the fact that the circumstances which necessitated the development and perpetuation of a Black American Theatre for a full century and a half still exist means that the tradition will be extended. But in an era of retrogressive social consciousness, will the Black Theatre lose the exuberance and that sense of social responsibility it had during the 1960s? As the new mood and present tendencies seem to indicate, the Black Theatre is becoming more unilateral. With Baraka denouncing Black Nationalism as reactionary and shifting his position to a Marxist–Leninist–Mao Tse-tung revolutionary program, the less radical artists of the theatre now wield the most influence. Revealing of this present shift is an article that appeared in the *New York Times* for April 29, 1979. The article, entitled "Black Theatre Has Moved Beyond Revolution," is a report on a festival of Black plays, some totally new and a few revivals, that was showcased at Lincoln Center. But it is important that the writer of the article makes the following surmise: "What began as a militant revolutionary trust attending headline issues of the day, has evolved into a quiet exploration of personal themes and African and Afro-American culture."[7] Whatever conclusions can be made from this statement, the one thing that is still for certain is that the Black Theatre Movement in the United States, begun with the establishment of the African Grove in 1821–22, is still alive and active.

NOTES

1. "Seasons with the Negro Ensemble Company," *New York Times*, 2 March 1975, sec. 2, p. 5.

2. Owen Dodson, "Playwrights in Dark Glasses," *Negro Digest (Black World)* 17 (April 1968): 35.

3. Theodore R. Hudson, *From LeRoi Jones to Amiri Baraka* (Durham, N.C.: Duke University Press, 1973), p. 181.

4. Leland M. Griffin, "A Dramatistic Theory of the Rhetoric of Movements," in *Critical Responses to Kenneth Burke*, ed. William H. Rueckert (Minneapolis: University of Minnesota, 1969), p. 463.

5. Ed Bullins, Introduction to *The New Lafayette Theatre Presents*, ed. Ed Bullins (New York: Doubleday/Anchor Press, 1974), p. 4.

6. Sidney Finkelstein, *Existentialism and Alienation in American Literature* (New York: International Publishers, 1967).

7. Bernard Carragher, "Black Theatre Has Moved beyond Revolution," *New York Times*, 29 April 1979, sec. D, p. 21.

Bibliography

BOOKS

Abramson, Doris E. *Negro Playwrights in the American Theatre, 1925–1959*. New York: Columbia University Press, 1969.

Aranha, Ray. *My Sister, My Sister*. New York: Samuel French, 1973.

Aristotle. "The Poetic." In *European Theories of the Drama*. Edited by Barrett H. Clark. New York: Crown Publishers, 1958.

Artaud, Antonin. *The Theatre and Its Double*. New York: Grove Press, 1958.

Baldwin, James. *Blues for Mister Charlie*. New York: Dell Publishing Co., 1964.

Baraka, Imamu Amiri. *Four Black Revolutionary Plays*. Indianapolis: The Bobbs-Merrill Co., 1969.

———. *Jello*. Chicago: Third World Press, 1970.

———. *Raise, Race, Rays, Raze: Essays Since 1965*. New York: Random House, 1971.

———. "The Slave." In *17 Plays: Sophocles to Baraka*. Edited by Bernard F. Dukore. New York: Thomas Y. Crowell Co., 1976.

———. *The Motion of History and Other Plays*. New York: William Morrow and Co., 1978.

Barbour, Floyd B., ed. *The Black Power Revolt: A Collection of Essays*. New York: Collier Books, 1969.

Bass, Kingsley B., Jr. "We Righteous Bombers." In *New Plays from the Black Theatre*. Edited by Ed Bullins. New York: Bantam Books, 1969.

Benston, Kimberly, W. *Baraka: The Renegade and the Mask*. New Haven: Yale University Press, 1976.

Bigsby, C. W. E. *Confrontation and Commitment: A Study of Contemporary American Drama, 1959–1966.* Columbia: University of Missouri Press, 1968.

————. ed. *The Black American Writer, Volume II: Poetry and Drama.* Baltimore: Penguin Books, 1969.

Bullins, Ed. *Five Plays By Ed Bullins.* Indianapolis/New York: The Bobbs-Merrill Co., 1968.

————. "How Do You Do? A Nonsense Drama." In *Black Fire: An Anthology of Afro-American Writing.* Edited by LeRoi Jones and Larry Neal. New York: Doubleday/Anchor Press, 1969.

————. Introduction to *The New Lafayette Theatre Presents.* Edited by Ed Bullins. Indianapolis/New York: The Bobbs-Merrill Co., 1974.

————. "The So-Called Western Avant-Garde Drama." In *Black Expression: Essays by and about Black Americans in the Creative Arts.* Edited by Addison Gayle, Jr. New York: Weybright and Talley, 1969.

————. ed. "The Gentleman Caller." In *A Black Quartet.* Edited by Clayton Riley. New York: New American Library/A Mentor Book, 1970.

————. *The Theme Is Blackness: The Corner and Other Plays.* New York: William Morrow and Co., 1973.

Caldwell, Ben. "Prayer Meeting Or the First Militant Preacher." In *A Black Quartet.* Introduction by Clayton Riley. New York: New American Library/A Mentor Book, 1970.

Carmichael, Stokely, and Hamilton, Charles V. *Black Power: The Politics of Liberation in America.* New York: Random House/Vintage Books, 1967.

Casebier, Allan. *Film Appreciation.* New York: Harcourt, Brace Jovanovich, 1976.

Cesaire, Aime. *A Season in the Congo.* New York: Grove Press/Evergreen Edition, 1969.

Couch, William, Jr., ed. *New Black Playwrights.* Baton Rouge: Louisiana State University Press, 1969.

Cruse, Harold. *The Crisis of the Negro Intellectual.* New York: William Morrow and Co., 1967.

————. *Rebellion or Revolution?* New York: William Morrow and Co., 1969.

Dean, Philip Hayes. *The Sty of the Blind Pig and Other Plays.* Indianapolis: The Bobbs-Merrill Co., 1973.

Dent, Thomas C.; Moses, Gil; and Schechner, Richard, eds. *The Free Southern Theater.* Indianapolis: The Bobbs-Merrill Co., 1969.

Draper, Theodore. *The Rediscovery of Black Nationalism.* New York: The Viking Press, 1970.

Eisenstein, Sergei. *Film Form.* New York: Harcourt, Brace and World/A Harvest Book, 1949.

Esslin, Martin. *The Theatre of the Absurd.* Garden City: Doubleday/Anchor Books, 1969.

Fanon, Frantz. *Wretched of the Earth.* New York: Grove Press, 1965.

———. *Black Skin, White Masks.* New York: Grove Press, 1967.

Finkelstein, Sidney. *Existentialism and Alienation in American Literature.* New York: International Publishers, 1967.

Garrett, Jimmy. "We Own the Night." In *Black Fire: An Anthology of Afro-American Writing.* Edited by LeRoi Jones and Larry Neal. New York: William Morrow and Co., 1971.

Gayle, Addison, Jr. *Black Expression.* New York: Weybright and Talley, 1970.

———. ed. *The Black Aesthetic.* New York: Doubleday/Anchor Books, 1971.

———. *The Way of the New World: The Black Novel in America.* New York: Doubleday/Anchor Books, 1975.

Genet, Jean. *The Blacks: A Clown Show.* New York: Grove Press, 1960.

Gerald, Carolyn. "The Black Writer and His Role." In *The Black Aesthetic.* Edited by Addison Gayle, Jr. New York: Doubleday/Anchor Books, 1972.

Gordone, Charles. *No Place to Be Somebody: A Black-Black Comedy.* New York: Samuel French, 1969.

Griffin, Leland M. "A Dramatic Theory of the Rhetoric of Movements." In *Critical Responses to Kenneth Burke.* Edited by William H. Rueckert. Minneapolis: University of Minnesota Press, 1969.

Harrier, Richard. Foreword to *Underground: Four Plays by Edgar White.* New York: William Morrow and Co., 1970.

Harrison, Paul Carter. *The Drama of Nommo: Black Theater in the African Continuum.* New York: Grove Press, 1972.

Hatch, James V., and Shine, Ted, eds. *Black Theatre USA: 45 Plays by Black Americans, 1847–1974.* New York: The Free Press, 1974.

Hernton, Calvin C. "Dynamite Growing Out of Their Heads." In *Black Fire: An Anthology of Afro-American Writing.* Edited by LeRoi Jones and Larry Neal. New York: William Morrow and Co., 1971.

Hill, Errol, ed. *The Theater of Black Americans, Volumes I and II.* Englewood Cliffs, N.J.: Prentice-Hall, 1980.

Hudson, Theodore R. *From LeRoi Jones to Amiri Baraka.* Durham, N.C.: Duke University Press, 1973.

Huggins, Nathan Irvin. *Harlem Renaissance*. New York: Oxford University Press, 1971.

Jahn, Janheinz. *Muntu: The New African Culture*. New York: Grove Press, 1961.

Johnson, James Weldon. *Black Manhattan*. New York: Arno Press and The New York Times, 1968.

Jones, LeRoi (Amiri Baraka). *Blues People*. New York: William Morrow and Co., 1963.

———. "Great Goodness of Life (A Coon Show)." In *A Black Quartet*. Edited by Clayton Riley. New York: New American Library/A Mentor Book, 1970.

Jones, LeRoi, and Neal, Larry, eds. *Black Fire: An Antholgoy of Afro-American Writing*. New York: William Morrow and Co., 1971.

Jones, Reginald L., ed. *Black Psychology*. New York: Harper and Row, 1972.

Karenga, Maulana Ron. "From the Quotable Karenga." In *The Black Power Revolt: A Collection of Essays*. Edited by Floyd B. Barbour. New York: Collier Books, 1968.

Kennedy, Adrienne. "Funnyhouse of a Negro." In *Anthology of the American Negro in the Theatre*. Edited by Lindsay Patterson. New York: Publishers Co., 1967.

———. "A Rat's Mass." In *New Black Playwrights*. Edited by William Couch, Jr. Baton Rouge: Louisiana State University Press, 1969.

———. "Sun: A Poem Inspired by the Death of Malcolm X." In *Spontaneous Combustion: Eight New American Plays*. Edited by Rochelle Owens. New York: Winter House, 1972.

———. *Black Theatre: Present Condition*. New York: Publishing Center for Cultural Resources, 1981.

Lahr, John. *Up Against the Fourth Wall: Essays on Modern Theatre*. New York: Grove Press, 1970.

———. *Astonish Me: Adventures in Contemporary Theater*. New York: The Viking Press, 1973.

Lahr, John, and Price, Jonathan, eds. *The Great American Life Show: 9 Plays from the Avant-Garde Theatre*. New York: Bantam Books, 1974.

Leab, Daniel J. *From Sambo to Superspade: The Black Experience in Motion Pictures*. Boston: Houghton Mifflin Co., 1976.

Lee, Leslie. *The First Breeze of Summer*. New York: Samuel French, 1975.

Lenin, V. I. *On Literature and Art*. Moscow: Progress Publishers, 1978.

Little, Stuart W. *Off-Broadway: The Prophetic Theatre*. New York: Coward, McCann and Geoghegan, 1972.

Littlejohn, David. *Black on White: A Critical Survey of Writings by American Negroes*. New York: Grossman Publishers, 1966.

Locke, Alain, ed. *The New Negro*. New York: Atheneum, 1977.

Locke, Alain, and Gregory, Montgomery, eds., *Plays of Negro Life: A Source of Native American Drama*. Westport, Conn.: Negro Universities Press, 1970.

Lunacharsky, Anatoly V. "Theses on the Problems of Marxist Criticism." In *Dramatic Theory and Criticism: Greeks to Grotowsky*. Edited by Bernard F. Dukore. New York: Holt, Rinehart and Winston, 1974.

Marcuse, Herbert. *Counterrevolution and Revolt*. Boston: Beacon Press, 1972.

Mayfield, Julian. "You Touch My Black Aesthetic and I'll Touch Yours." In *The Black Aesthetic*. Edited by Addison Gayle, Jr. New York: Doubleday/Anchor Books, 1972.

Milner, Ron. "The Warning—A Theme for Linda." In *A Black Quartet*. Edited by Clayton Riley. New York: New American Library/A Mentor Book, 1970.

Mitchell, Loften. *Black Drama: The Study of the American Negro in the Theatre*. New York: Hawthorn Books, 1967.

———. *Voices of the Black Theatre*. Clifton, N.J.: James T. White and Co., 1975.

Novack, George, ed. *Existentialism Versus Marxism: Conflicting Views in Humanism*. New York: Dell Publishing Co./A Delta Book, 1966.

Patterson, Lindsay, ed. *Black Theatre: A 20th Century Collection of the Works of Its Best Playwrights*. New York: New American Library/A Plume Book, 1971.

Reardon, William R., and Pawley, Thomas D. *The Black Teacher and the Dramatic Arts: A Dialogue, Bibliography, and Anthology*. Westport, Conn.: Negro Universities Press, 1970.

Ross, Laura, ed., *Theatre Profiles 5*. New York: Theatre Communications Group, 1982.

Sainer, Arthur. *The Radical Theatre Notebook*. New York: Avon Books/Discus Books, 1975.

Sanchez, Sonia. "Sister Son/ji." In *New Plays from the Black Theatre*. Edited by Ed Bullins. New York: Bantam Books, 1969.

Shange, Ntozake. *For Colored Girls Who Have Considered Suicide When the Rainbow is Enuf*. New York: Macmillan Co., 1977.

Sollors, Werner. *Amiri Baraka—LeRoi Jones*. New York: Columbia University Press, 1978.

Turner, Darwin T., ed. *Black Drama in America*. Greenwich, Conn.: Fawcett Premier Book, 1971.

Walker, Joseph A. *The River Niger*. New York: Samuel French, 1973.

Ward, Douglas Turner. "Day of Absence." In *New Black Playwrights*.

Edited by William Couch, Jr. Baton Rouge: Louisiana State University Press, 1969.

Wesley, Richard. "Black Terror: A Revolutionary Adventure Story." In *The New Lafayette Theatre Presents*. Edited by Ed Bullins, New York: Doubleday/Anchor Press, 1974.

White, Edgar. *Underground: Four Plays by Edgar White*. New York: William Morrow and Co., 1970.

———. *The Crucificado: Two Plays by Edgar White*. New York: William Morrow and Co., 1973.

Wilson, Robert J. *The Black Theatre Alliance: A History of Its Founding Members*. Unpublished Ph.D Dissertation. New York: Schomburg Collection.

Wright, Richard. *The Outsider*. New York: Harper and Row/Perennial Library, 1966.

PERIODICALS

Abeke. "Van Peebles: On the Inside." *Essence* (June 1973).

Allen, Bonnie. "Black Theatre Alliance: United for Excellence." *Essence* (November 1977).

Bailey, Peter. "The Importance of Being Black." *Newsweek* (24 February 1969).

———. "The Black Theatre: Artists Take Revolutionary Works to Community." *Ebony* (25 August 1969).

———. "Melvin Van Peebles' 'Natural Death' Called Effective." *Jet Magazine* (18 November 1971).

———. "Annual Round-Up, Black Theater in America: New York." *Black World* (April 1972).

———. "Woodie King, Jr.: Renaissance Man of Black Theater." *Black World* (April 1975).

———. "Black Theatre Festival—U.S.A." *Ebony* (October 1979).

Baraka, Amiri. "In Search of the Revolutionary Theatre." *Black World* (April 1966).

———. "Black Revolutionary Poets Should Also Be Playwrights." *Black World* (April 1972).

Black Theatre: A Periodical of the Black Theatre Movement, nos. 5 and 6, 1971–72.

Bond, Carey. "For Colored Girls who have Considered Suicide." *Freedomways* (November 1976).

Bontemps, Alex. "Bubbling Brown Sugar: A Musical about Harlem Tells the History of Black Entertainment." *Ebony* (February 1976).

Brecht, Stefen. "LeRoi Jones' *Slave Ship*." *Drama Review* (Winter 1970).

Bullins, Ed. "Theatre of Reality." *Black World* (April 1966).
————. "On Street Theatre." *Tulane Drama Review* (Summer 1968).
Coleman, Michael. "What Is Black Theatre? An Interview with Imamu Amiri Baraka." *Black World* (April 1971).
Davis, Curt. " 'Bubbling Brown Sugar' Doesn't Quite Boil." *Encore American and Worldwide News* (19 April 1976).
————. "The Negro Ensemble Company's Decade of Drama." *Encore American and Worldwide News* (22 November 1976).
————. "Springer-Time on Broadway." *Encore American and Worldwide News* (20 December 1976).
Dodson, Owen. "Playwrights in Dark Glasses." *Negro Digest (Black World)* (April 1968).
Du Bois, W. E. B. " 'Krigwa Players Little Negro Theatre': The Story of a Little Theatre Movement." *Crisis* (July 1926).
Gaffney, Floyd. "The Free Southern Theater: Not Just Survival." *Crisis* (January 1978).
Gussow, Mel. "The Baadassss Success of Melvin Van Peebles." *New York Times Magazine* (20 August 1972).Harris, Jessica. "Broadway's New Breed: Our Producers on the Great White Way." *Essence* (December 1977).
Hay, Samuel A. "African-American Drama, 1950–1970." *Negro History Bulletin* (October 1972).
Higgins, Chester. "Meet the Man behind 'Sweetback' Movie." *Jet Magazine* (1 July 1971).
Horton, Joseph. "Cable Car Pilots." *Sepia* (November 1972).
Jaynes, Julian. "The Lost Voices of Gods: Reflections on the Dawn of Consciousness." *Psychology Today* (November 1977).
Jeyifous, Abiodun. "Black Critics on Black Theatre." *Drama Review* (September 1974).
Johnson, James Weldon. "The Dilemma of the Negro Writer." *American Mercury* (December 1928).
Kalem, T. E. "Jumping Jivernacular: 'The Wiz.' " *Time* (20 January 1975).
Kisner, Ronald. " 'Wine-Sellers': Pimps, Prostitutes Play Big Draw." *Jet Magazine* (15 May 1975).
Kroll, Jack. "Oz with Soul." *Newsweek* (20 January 1975).
————. " 'No Place to Be Somebody'—Powerful Black Play." *Newsweek* (2 June 1969).
Leakey, Richard, and Lewin, Roger. "Origins of the Mind." *Psychology Today* (July 1978).
Martin, Sharon Stockard. "The Tanning of Oz: Reflections on the Usurpation of a Myth." *Essence* (September 1975).

Miller, Adam David. "It's a Long Way to St. Louis: Notes on the Audience for Black Drama." *Tulane Drama Review* (Summer 1968).

Millroy, Marilyn. "Vivian Robinson: Giving Black Theater a Boost." *Essence* (September 1982).

Morrison, Allan. "100 Years of Negro Entertainment." *Ebony* (September 1963).

Neal, Larry. "The Black Arts Movement." *Tulane Drama Review* (Summer 1968).

"Negro Ensemble Company Lives On." *Africa* (July 1980).

Pawley, Thomas D. "The Black Theatre Audience." *Players* (August–September 1971).

———. "The First Black Playwrights." *Black World* (April 1972).

Peterson, Maurice. "Ain't Supposed to Die a Natural Death." *Essence* (February 1972).

———. "The Wiz's Wizzes: Ken Harper." *Essence* (September 1975).

———. "On the Road with the Wine-Sellers." *Essence* (November 1975).

Prideaux, Tom. "A Loving, Healing Kind of Theater." *Life* (September 1966).

Salaam, Kalamu ya. "Making the Image Real: Black Producers of Theater, Film and Television." *Black Collegian* (March–April 1977).

Schroeder, R. J. "The Free Southern Theater." *Commonweal* (18 March 1966).

"Stage, Screen and Black Hegemony: The Black World Interviews Woodie King, Jr." *Black World* (April 1975).

Steele, Shelby. " 'White Port and Lemon Juice': Notes on Ritual in the New Black Theatre." *Black World* (June 1973).

Sutherland, Elizabeth. "Theatre of the Meaningful." *Nation* (19 October 1964).

Taylor, Clarke. "In the Theatre of Soul." *Essence* (April 1975).

Teer, Barbara Ann. "The Great White Way Is Not Our Way—Not Yet." *Negro Digest (Black World)* (April 1968).

Walcott, Ronald. "Ellison, Gordone and Tolson: Some Notes on the Blues, Style and Space." *Black World* (December 1972).

Weathers, Diane. "Curtain Up on Broadway's Newest Star—Black Producer." *Black Enterprise* (December 1977).

Williams, Paulette. "Barbara Ann Teer: Producer." *Ebony* (August 1977).

NEWSPAPERS

Barnes, Clive. "Blacks Move through Gantlet of Slum." *New York Times*, 21 October 1971, p. 55.

———. " 'Don't Play Us Cheap' a Fun Comedy Musical." *New York Times* 17 May 1972, p. 39.

———. " 'The Wiz' (Of Oz): Black Musical Shows Vitality and Style." *New York Times*, 6 January 1975, sec. L, p. 32.

———. " 'Bubbling Brown Sugar' Boils at ANTA." *New York Times*, 3 March 1976, p. 30.

———. "The Guy Who's Rocking the Boat." *New York Times*, 23 June 1976, sec. 3, p. 3.

———. "Goodspeed Company Presents Musical." *New York Times*, 30 June 1976, p. 22.

———. "New 'Guys and Dolls' Comes Seven Again." *New York Times*, 22 July 1976, p.26.

Blau, Eleanor. "The Negro Ensemble Company Is on the Move." *New York Times*, 31 August 1980, sec. D., p. 3.

Buckley, Tom. "The Big Bucks of Show Biz on Broadway." *Houston Chronicle*, 7 May 1978, p. 25.

Carragher, Bernard. "Black Theater Has Moved beyond Revolution." *New York Times*, 29 April 1979, sec. D., p. 21.

Cummings, Judith. "Blacks Gain on Broadway; Lag in 2 Other Arts." *New York Times*, 6 June 1975, p. 10.

Giovanni, Nikki. "I Get a Charge from Seeing Myself on Stage." *New York Times*, 28 May 1972, sec. 3, p. 1.

Gussow, Mel. "Casting by Race Can Be Touchy." *New York Times*, 1 August 1976, sec. 2, p. 5.

———. " 'Going Up' Is a Musical Charmer." *New York Times*, 20 September 1976, p. 39.

———. "Williams' '16th Round': A Fighter's Finish." *New York Times*, 10 October 1980.

Hill, Marshall. "Melvin Van Peebles—A Black Exploiter?" Letter to the editor, *New York Times Magazine*, September 10, 1972, p. 33.

Kerr, Walter. "Mr. Bullins Is Himself at Fault." *New York Times*, 19 March 1972, sec. D., p. 1.

———. "RX for 'Going Up': Three Edward Everett Hortons." *New York Times*, 18 July 1976, sec. 2, p. 1.

Lester, Elenore. " 'We Exist to Create a Real Black Theatre': Seasons with the Negro Ensemble Company." *New York Times*, 2 March 1975, sec. 2, p. 5.

McQuiston, John T. " 'The Wiz,' Best Musical, Wins 7 Tonys." *New York Times*, 17 August 1970, p. 42.

Novick, Julius. "The Taking of Miss Cegnation (A Review): 'The Taking of Miss Janie.' " *Village Voice*, 12 May 1975.

Phillips, McCandlish. "In Summer, Shows Take to the Streets." *New York Times*, 27 August 1970, p. 42.

———. "Message of Street Theatre Is Strong." *New York Times*, 22 June 1971, p. 28.

Riley, Clayton. "We Will Not Be a New Form of White Art in Black Face." *New York Times*, 14 June 1970.

Rollins, Bryant. "Does 'The Wiz' Say Something Extra to Blacks?" *New York Times*, 28 December 1975, sec. 2, p. 5.

Tapley, Mel. "Barbara Ann Teer Revisits Africa." *Amsterdam News*, 1980.

Ward, Douglas Turner. "American Theatre: For Whites Only?" *New York Times*, 14 August 1966.

Weiler, A. H. "Melvin Van Prolific." *New York Times*, 28 May 1972, p. 9.

INTERVIEWS

Martin, Sharon Stockard. Interviewed August 13, 1983, in Nashville, Tennessee. Martin has been a member of the Ed Bullins Black Theatre Workshop (1968–69), the FST Writer's Workshop (1970–73), the Frank Silvera Writer's Workshop (1973–76), the Congo Square Writers (1976–79), and the L.A. Actors Theatre Playwright Workshop (1980). Martin's published plays are *Proper and Fine* and *Fanny Lou Hamer's Entourage*.

O'Neal, John. Interviewed via telephone, September 24, 1983, New Orleans, Louisiana. O'Neal worked in the Civil Rights Movement in the South in the early 1960s and was a field secretary for the Student Nonviolent Coordinating Committee. In 1963 he co-founded the Free Southern Theater, which for almost twenty years sought to be "a theater for those who have no theater" by touring throughout the Black Belt South. He now works as a director, teacher, and playwright, as well as a performer. O'Neal was the principal administrator of the Free Southern Theater for most of its nineteen years.

Shine, Ted. Interviewed October 20, 21, and 22, 1983, in Nashville, Tennessee. A prolific writer for television and stage, many of Dr. Shine's plays have been performed in southern colleges and universities as well as Off-Broadway and by the Negro Ensemble Company in New York City. A native of Dallas, Texas, Shine has taught at Dillard and Howard universities and is currently Chairman of the Theatre Department at Prairie View University in Prairie View, Texas. Shine's plays include *Contribution*, *Herbert III*, *Shoes*, and *Baby Cakes*.

Turner, Charles. Interviewed March 31 and April 1, and 2, 1983, in

Nashville, Tennessee. Turner is a New York–based ac-
tor/director. He has directed for the Hartford Stage Company,
the American Place Festival, the Lincoln Center Outdoor Festival, the Player's State Theatre, and some of the leading colleges
and universities in the United States. He recently staged A. R.
Gurney's *Scenes from American Life* for S.U.N.Y. at Purchase, New
York. Moreover, Turner is the recipient of the Ninth Annual
Audelco Recognition Award for Achievement in Direction of a
Musical. He directed Ed Schockley's *Bessie Smith, Empress of the
Blues* in the spring of 1983, which ran for thirteen S.R.O. weeks
at the Frank Silvera Writer's Workshop Theatre.

OTHER

Black Theatre Alliance, Newsletter No. 1. Schomburg Collection, Schom-
     burg Center for Research in Black Culture, New York.
Gordone, Charles. *The Black Experience in the Arts.* Filmstrip produced
     and edited by Lilla Brownstone. Pleasantville, N.Y.: Warren
     Schloat Productions, 1971.
Historical Precis, New Lafayette Theatre. Schomburg Center Clipping
     File, Schomburg Center for Research in Black Culture, New York.
     Microfilm.
McBeth, Robert. *Black Theatre: An on the Spot Report,* Lafayette Theatre.
     Schomburg Center Clipping File, Schomburg Center for Re-
     search in Black Culture, New York. Microfilm.
————. "Statement," from the program of the New Lafayette Inau-
     gural Season, 1967–68. Schomburg Center for Research in Black
     Culture, New York. Microfilm.
The New Lafayette Theatre. *Historical Precis.* Schomburg Center Clip-
     ping File. Schomburg Center for Research in Black Culture, New
     York. Microfilm.

Index

About the Author

MANCE WILLIAMS was Assistant Professor in the Department of
Dramatics and Speech at Fisk University, Nashville. He was the author of "Criticism of Black Fiction," published in *Man and His Awareness*.